SURVIVORS OF THE DARK REBELLION

GOD'S HEROES
FROM ADAM TO DAVID

SALLY PIERSON DILLON

REVIEW AND HERALD® PUBLISHING ASSOCIATION
Since 1861 | www.reviewandherald.com

The Review and Herald® Publishing Association publishes biblically-based materials for spiritual, physical, and mental growth and Christian discipleship.

The author assumes full responsibility for the accuracy of all facts and quotations as cited in this book.

This book was
Edited by Gerald Wheeler
Cover designed by Trent Truman
Electronic makeup by Shirley M. Bolivar
Cover art by Greg and Tim Hildebrandt
Typeset: Berkeley Book 12/16

Printed by Pacific Press® Publishing Association
PRINTED IN U.S.A.

Library of Congress Cataloging-in-Publication Data
Dillon, Sally Pierson, 1959-2007.
  Survivors of the dark rebellion: God's heroes from Adam to David / Sally Pierson Dillon.
    p. cm.
  ISBN 978-0-8280-1686-5
  1. Bible. O.T—History of Biblical events—Juvenile works. 2. Bible. O.T—History of Biblical events 3. Good and evil—Juvenile works. 4. Good and evil. I. Title.

PZ7.D5797 Sur 2002
220.9
                          2005273363

Other books by Sally Pierson Dillon include:
    Hugs From Jesus
    Little Hearts for Jesus
    Michael Asks Why

To order, call **1-800-765-6955.**

June 2019

DEDICATION

To Melinda and Josh, who are also survivors of the Dark Rebellion
and continue to live and love and prove that His love conquers all.

To the love of my life, whose support and encouragement
combined with his eccentric sense of humor made
this project possible, fulfilling, and fun.

To Denice, Mike, Betty, Kelly, Jeannette, Kathy, and Gerald—
who brought order from chaos and made this book possible.

Main Characters

MARK	Recording angel and observer, heaven
SHEENA	Daughter of Adam and Eve, Eden
NALA	Visits Noah's building project
TERAH	Son of Eliazar, servant of Abraham, Canaan
ASENATH	Daughter of the high priest of On, Egypt
MAHLEENDAH	Sister of Zipporah
SENEFRU	Son of a metalworker, Egypt, great-grandson of Abraham
TIRZAH	Sister of Heber, a metalworker, Canaan, granddaughter of Senefru
JOAB	Volunteer in Gideon's army to fight the Midianites
JARED	Student in the Schools of the Prophets

MARK

his is a time of great secrets, and I am almost bursting with mine. The Son of the Mighty One met with me earlier and told me of many changes coming to my life. He said my human name would be Mark. What's a human? That was not one of the secrets He shared with me except that sometime later He will call me by that title.

My role is going to change too. Until now I have just been part of the group of angels who tended the heavenly gardens, and, of course, I was part of the mass choir. The high point of our existence has been when we all sing under our high commander Lucifer's direction and find new harmonies and new and exciting ways to praise the Mighty One.

Now I am to be an invisible watcher and will record what I observe. I'm not sure why this is important. Invisible to whom? The Mighty One explained to me that humans, once they come into being, might not be able to see me unless I specifically materialize to be visible in the part of the light spectrum that their vision registers. I guess I'll have to see a human really to understand this, but I am to start keeping records now. The Mighty One taught me the heavenly record-keeping system we are to use with all of it's complicated cross-referencing and archiving. Then He will have me start extracting from it various segments to make a short and readable record for humans. He said that later it would be very helpful to them. So humans, whatever and whoever you are, I am starting this record for you. Perhaps both of us will understand better what the Mighty One has planned as these secrets unfold. In the meantime, it's very exciting.

My record-keeping system has more aspects than I understand right now. One whole section is called forgiveness and atonement. The Son of the Almighty gave me a brief explanation, but He said that it was something I will learn about more fully later. He explained that it involved transferring records to a central place and then in atonement they would be wiped out completely. When I couldn't understand it, the Son of the Most High just laughed melodiously and said that it was a beautiful component but that hopefully I would not have to use it anytime in the future.

Later I asked Lucifer about it, hoping that perhaps he could give me a little more information. He just frowned and said that he didn't think it was fair that we received tasks to do and equipment to use that we weren't given full explanations for. His reaction shocked me, and I had to think about it for a few minutes. What surprised me the most was not that the Mighty One would not give me a full explanation, for there are probably many things in His mind that He has not revealed to us, but that Lucifer did not know the answer and seemed to be disturbed by the fact. Perhaps the Mighty One was planning more briefings for our commander-in-chief so that he would understand all of the components of the systems He had placed his underlings in charge of.

As a record keeper, the Son of the Mighty One told me, I would have access to all the other angel groups involved. It is His big project, and yet He is letting each of us have a part in the plan! I feel greatly honored. It makes me want to just fly pirouettes about Him and shout my gratitude in songs of worship. But then I caught

Lucifer's eye. Something odd is going on here, but I don't know what it is. Perhaps I will find out if I continue my investigation.

I went to visit my friends working on the light project. The Son of the Almighty helped them simulate a nitrogenous atmosphere with specific proportions of oxygen and carbon dioxide and other such elements, and then they experimented with different wavelengths of the electromagnetic spectrum shining through it. They will be selecting the wavelengths to use on this new project. My friends don't know whether to think of themselves as scientists or artists. They are working on developing the very structures of the new environment the Son is going to create. He will do the actual creating, but He is allowing them to see the kinds of things He will have to bring into existence to make His plan complete.

We all felt much laughter and excitement as I talked with each friend and recorded their findings. However, as Lucifer came through, he seemed less enthusiastic. When I asked him about it he just shrugged and said that as the angel of light, he felt the Son was not using the appropriate chain of command since light was specifically his department. Those of us who heard his comment just stared at him openmouthed. Everything he said was true, but the Son had a right to be in charge of any creative project He wanted to. I didn't understand Lucifer's problem, but then politics is not my strong area. I am a recorder, so I guess I will start watching and recording and try to figure out why he is less excited about this project than all of the rest of us.

My botanist friends were having a wonderful time. The Son had visited them and given them a wide range of not only atmospheric conditions, but temperatures and ranges in humidity for them to work with. They were drawing up plans for different botany life forms that could thrive in each area. Angels helped with the plans for the life forms too. Although the Son could have thought up every detail of what He intended to create and would bring them into actual existence, He let us, His servants, participate in the planning. He would announce the kind of thing He would make, then let us work out some of the characteristics it might have.

Today a group of angels were working on air-breathing creatures, each discussing the percentage of oxygen in the air, the atmospheric pressure, and the lungs that would be needed. Apparently a lung is something inside of a life form that makes them able to absorb the oxygen into their bodies. The oxygen forms part of the chemical process that makes such creatures live. The angels estimated the total surface area it would take for enough oxygen to cross to sustain different sized life forms and then figured out how to shrink that huge surface area down into something that would fit inside a small animal.

The Son could have designed it all by Himself, but He wanted to allow us to think along with Him. Of course only He could do all the details and actually bring the various plants and animals to life.

The angels working on the concept of breathing organs for the larger organisms came up with a concept that resembled the cluster of grapes that the botanists were thinking about, except, of course, this would be lung tissue, not plant tissue. It all looked fascinating to me. In another part of the botanists' area I found a genetics team at work. What they were doing was even harder for me to understand, but apparently the creatures in this new project, while they will be created from the hand of the Son just as my friends and I were, He is actually going to put within them the ability to re-create their own kind—and not just exact reproductions but a whole range of variations that reflect the characteristics of the two parent creatures. The concept astounded me. We had seen nothing like this before. All of us had been individually handcrafted by the Son of the Most High Himself.

Lucifer shook his head. "It amazes me," he said, "that the Most High wants to give His creative power to these lower beings He's

planning to make, and not just to the humans who apparently will
be the smartest beings in the project. Every creature down to the
lowliest crawling thing will share the ability. They will be able to re-
produce themselves without any assistance."

"But surely," I interrupted, "surely they will know that all life
comes from the Mighty One and that without Him giving life to
each reproduction, it would just be lifeless matter."

The covering cherub snorted. "I doubt if they'll be that bright."

I felt confused. Lucifer was my supreme commander, and I
loved him and respected him. Never before had I sensed even an
inkling of dissent between him and the Mighty Ones. What was
happening? Had it been there before and I had just been unaware,
or was there something about the new project that upset him?
Surely, even if he had questions, he would be supportive of the
Mighty One's plan. It would not be the first time that we had not
understood everything, and yet when the Mighty Ones completed
their plans, they were always perfect. What was the problem?

As I spoke to Ariel, he shared some of the concerns that Lucifer
had mentioned to him. Was it really fair of God to ask us to help
with some of the research for His new project and not explain what
it was? How could we do adequate research without knowing, and
was it really right for Him to take our work and assume credit for it
all when He put the finished product together and created what we
had worked on together?

"Of course it's fair," I laughed. "He's our God! The Mighty One
has a huge master plan. We are only small parts of it. And all of us
together do not know enough to completely design it, least of all
make things live."

Ariel looked at me and smiled. "That's true. I don't know what
I was thinking. It's just when I talk to Lucifer—well, he seems so
angry, and yet when I'm with him everything he says makes sense
and it seems that he is only seeking to be treated fairly."

I shook my head. "The Mighty One has always been fair to us, so why would we suspect Him of anything else now?" Ariel nodded. "I don't always understand what He's doing," I continued, "but I love Him and trust Him, and He has never ever given me reason not to."

"Perhaps," Ariel suggested, "Lucifer is just feeling upset because the Mighty Ones are not including him in the plans for this new project."

Thinking it over, I slowly nodded in agreement.

"Should he be?" Ariel asked. "I mean, he is our commander-in-chief."

I shrugged. "I don't know. But this is the Almighty One's universe, so if it is His choice to do the project with the Son and the Spirit and not with Lucifer, I guess He has a right to decide that."

"What is sad to me," Ariel whispered, "is that it is causing division among us. Many have become suspicious of the Mighty One. It gives me an anxious feeling. We've never had that here before. This has always been a place of harmony. I don't like it. I saw the Son walking with Lucifer, talking intensely with him. I hope they work things out, because if they don't, I have a feeling something terrible will happen."

Indeed, something terrible did happen. For a time Lucifer seemed undecided about what he should do. During our praise services he would lead us in the most beautiful anthems to the Mighty One and truly seemed to mean what he sang—and yet his questions continued. The bitterness became overwhelming until finally the Mighty One had to summon him into the throne room and ask him to choose whether he would remain loyal to the Three or persist in sowing dissension in heaven. When he refused to stop, war broke out in heaven, and the Mighty Ones had to expel all of Lucifer's followers. It was a time of great heartbreak. Even those of us who loved the Father with great passion felt too sad to sing, which was all right, for the Father was in tears too. How could this have happened? And what disaster would take place next?

"Ariel," I asked, "do you think the Mighty One will destroy Lucifer?"

The other angel shook his head. "No, I believe that if He was going to do that, it would have happened by now. Lucifer has accused Him of being unfair and has said that He is not a good leader and that he, Lucifer, would do a much better job. Perhaps the Mighty One is going to let him have an opportunity in some limited way to show us just what life would be like if Lucifer was in charge."

"That could be," I said after considering it for a while. "Our Mighty One is wise, for if He just destroyed Lucifer, we would never know for sure if Lucifer's claims were right or not. This way we will see exactly what happens, and in all fairness, He is giving Lucifer an opportunity to show us."

"Yes. But I feel so badly about all of this. I feel so torn between them. Lucifer was our commander, and I loved him. And I love the Almighty One too."

"Maybe," I suggested, "if Lucifer does a good job wherever it is the Mighty One sends him, perhaps there can be some reconciliation between them later."

Ariel raised an eyebrow. "You really think so?" he asked, then shook his head. None of us knew, but every one of us had had to make a choice of loyalties. I had chosen the Mighty One. Now we had to see how things turned out in the struggle that we began to call the great controversy.

MARK

fter our daily praises the Son rose to make an announcement. His eyes sparkled as He said, "The plans are all complete, and now We will share them with you. We are going to create Planet Earth. We will give it its own sun and small solar system to revolve in. Its inhabitants will use them to mark time. And all its creatures from the highest to the lowest will be capable of reproducing themselves."

Those who had not known of the Son's plans caught their breath in astonishment. It was not something that happened in heaven. How would that work? How wonderful to be a creature who could actually have a part in the creation like the Almighty! I felt a pang of sadness as I thought of Lucifer. Because of his jealousy and anger he would not be able to share in the excitement of the birth of this new world. But I couldn't think about that right now for the Son was still speaking.

"And you are all invited," He said. "We will be traveling to that part of the universe and you may watch the creation process." Spontaneously we broke into another song of praise. It had to be the most exciting thing that had happened since our own creation.

FIRST DAY

We hovered a safe distance out in space as we watched the Son prepare for the first creative act. Raising His hand, He spoke and a blinding explosion of light rippled across space. As our eyes adjusted, we noticed a water-covered planet turn slowly beneath us.

SECOND DAY

The next gathering we had the Son called "day two." Again He lifted His hands and spoke. We swooped in closer for a better look. Heavy clouds filled the planet's atmosphere. Already it had the right proportions of oxygen and other gases for its future inhabitants to breathe. It was becoming a world ready for life.

THIRD DAY

But if I thought what we had witnessed so far was exciting, the next day just took my breath away. This time when the Son spoke, land appeared. It was no longer an aquatic planet. He commanded again, and a carpet of green quickly materialized over the land, and then trees, shrubs, and flowers burst from the ground, bearing all kinds of fruit!

"Come join me," cried the Son. Down on the surface of the planet, He said, "In this area, I am creating a special garden. It will be the home of our first human creatures. This tree is a very special one. It is the celestial portal for this planet. You may have access to this planet anytime, those of you who are guardians, record keepers, or any of you who wish to visit. You may enter through here. Lucifer and the beings who joined him, they also have access to this planet through this port; but they have to stay at the tree as long as the inhabitants of this planet are loyal to Us.

We laughed. "Of course they'll be loyal. Why would they choose anything else?" Yet I had sensed a trace of sadness in the Son's voice. It puzzled me. Watching the Son of the Almighty create this world was the most exciting thing I had ever experienced. Shouldn't He be just as excited?

FOURTH DAY

On the fourth day we all sprawled out on the lush surface of the planet. The water droplets and other particulate matter in the oxygen-rich atmosphere started to settled. As it did, the air became clear. When the sun set below the horizon we could see the system's other planets and nearby stars. Amid all the oohs and ahs came a voice from the tree. The pouting presence there was almost palpable. "You know those stars were there all the time," Lucifer taunted. "He didn't just create them."

My friend Ariel laughed. "That is true." Ariel was one of the angels who specialized in astronomy and knew many of the planets from various missions in the service of the Almighty. "However," he said," what is beautiful about this is not that the planets were already here, but that the Creator made it so that the inhabitants of earth could see them. Now they will be able to use them to track time."

FIFTH DAY

We lay there marveling at the creative power of our God and laughing at the fun we had had so far watching Him. "You should have seen Aurora yesterday," Ariel continued. "When the Son spoke and all the trees started to grow, Aurora swooped in to get a closer look and then had to jump back immediately, because a branch had grown out to where his nose would have been."

I laughed and said that I wished I had seen that.

"I found out that we can fly backwards as fast as the Creator can make branches grow on earthly trees," Aurora commented, overhearing us.

"We have already made another scientific discovery," Ariel joked. "And now I can hardly wait to see what the Creator will do for day five."

Just as the sun began to peek over the horizon, He began to speak or to sing. A melodious lilt so filled His voice that we couldn't tell the difference. And in answer to Him, little winged creatures—not like us, but smaller with solid little bodies—flitted into existence. No, I guess you could not call them solid for they seemed not to weigh much, perhaps with hollow bones to be light enough so they could fly. Instantly they darted about and chirped and warbled back as He continued to sing. More and more varieties filled the air and the tree branches. I marveled at their differences. Some had short triangular beaks for pecking seeds.

"That's what they'll eat," the Creator explained when He saw us studying them. "Look at this one with his long, slender beak. He'll be able to get right into these flowers and drink the honey and nectar from them." Their colors and shapes were overwhelming.

"Was this the great masterpiece You have hinted about?" I asked.

He shook His head with a twinkle in His eye. "Oh, no, we're working up to that, but I'm glad you like the birds!"

"Come, look in the water," He said. As we dived in, we realized that the rivers and seas were no longer still but teaming with life. Beautiful silvery creatures swam past, then more kinds, all of various colors, sizes, textures. Each of their shapes differed as well. "This type of tail is for fast swimming," the Creator pointed out. "And these fins—this one's fins are small and thin and snakelike so he can rest in the cracks in the rocks," He continued to explain—and I just marveled. Many angels had worked at the labs learning about water dynamics and how different kinds of fins and other fish parts worked in the water. Yet none of us had seen a final design or put all the components together—to say nothing of viewing the creature with life of its own. Our Creator was awesome and we worshiped Him, bubbling our praises under the water. As we followed Him around oohing and aahing, it seemed no time until the light began disappearing from the sky and Day Five was over.

"Tomorrow," He said, "You will see My masterpiece." We could hardly wait.

SIXTH DAY

The Creator started very early on Day Six, hours before the sun cast a rosy dawn over the hills. "Why so early?" I asked Him.

He laughed. "Don't be fooled by the light and the darkness," He said. "Most humans will function during the light time and sleep during the darkness, but the darkness is hardly a time of inactivity. Many creatures will be active only at night and sleep in the daytime. Those are the ones I am creating now. Humans will call them nocturnal because of their habits." He spoke several more creatures into existence and then turned and looked at me. "What do you notice about these?"

I studied them. Each pair was a little different. And yet I did notice that apart from them having fur and four legs, two ears, and a tail, they had very large round eyes that gave a comical, cute expression. "Is it their eyes?" I asked.

"Their eyes will be bigger than some of the other animals because they will need to see in the darkness."

"They are perfect!" I exclaimed. "What are their names?"

The Creator paused. "I'm going to let Adam name them."

"Adam?"

"Ah, yes, Adam. You will have to wait a little bit to meet him. He is not here yet." Then He returned to His work, bringing more new pairs of creatures into existence.

Soon the light of the sun appeared over the brow of the hill. We all broke into spontaneous applause and songs of joy as we marveled at the beautiful colors streaking the sky. The Son smiled at us, acknowledging our appreciation, and then continued to create more beings. Our song of joy paused as we all started laughing at some of them.

A large pair of gray beasts with huge flapping ears and a long nose and a short, skinny little tail had wandered over to the fruit trees. One of them had reached up into the tree with his long, flexible nose (I wonder what Adam will call this one, anyway) and grabbed a piece of fruit. His mate grabbed him by the tail and pulled on it as if to say, "Now, don't get that fruit until you see if the Creator says it's OK for us to eat it." Turning, he made eye contact with her and flapped one of his ears. Just then a large yellow beast with long skinny legs and an even taller slender neck wandered over to the tree and began munching on leaves high in its branches. The first gray beast glanced at the second one and almost appeared to raise an eyebrow. She flapped her ears and let go of his tail, and they both helped themselves to fruit from the tree.

"Eat," the Creator said. "I made it for you." Soon animals, nosing around and exploring, digging in the fragrant earth or climbing in the trees, filled the hills and valleys. The Creator stopped, yet the day was only half over.

"I wonder which one is Adam?" I said to myself.

The Creator smiled and said nothing, but moved over to an area where He had a mound of damp clay. Kneeling, He scooped it into His hands and began to shape it into intricate forms.

"What is He doing?" Ariel inquired. "Doesn't He usually just speak things into existence?"

"Yes, He has so far." Of course it was hard to say what was usual for the Creator for this was all new to us. Although He heard us He did not answer. But His eyes twinkled as He continued to mold the clay. "He's making another beast," I exclaimed. "Look, He's creating it from the inside out."

"This will be a bony type structure, and these are organs and connective tissues," He explained. Soon He had covered those layers with muscles and other body tissues and then a smooth layer on the outside to protect it all. As He continued to mold the outer features, I caught my breath in amazement.

"It looks—it looks like Him!" I gasped. The other angels had noticed too. We all stared in amazement. Although it appeared to be a beast He was forming, it somehow resembled the Son of the Almighty One! Or what He would look like if He had a corporeal body. The Creator sat back and examined His work. Then gently He bent down and blew breath into the creature. Suddenly the clay figure began to take on a soft rosy hue.

"It's alive," I exclaimed at the same instant as the rest of my friends. We caught our breath in amazement. And it was! The hair on his head now rippled as he turned his head to the side. His chest rose and fell as he continued to breathe on his own. His eyelids fluttered open as he stared into the face of his Creator.

"Good morning, Adam," the Creator said to him. The being smiled. "Adam," the Son repeated. "Yes, that is your name. You are man." We all applauded and cheered as the human rose to his feet. "I created this home for you," the Creator continued, leading Adam by the hand. "You are the prince of this planet. Many creatures live here. You will be the king of everything. Take good care of them and this garden home, and they will be your companions."

Adam's face glowed with delight as he discovered each surprise. The Creator chuckled with glee along with the human, and we all joined in. It was the most fun we had had all week. Suddenly on impulse Adam broke into a run, following some creatures about half his size who scampered up into a tree and swung from branch to branch. "Stop, stop," the Creator laughed. "You are their prince, remember? Call them, and they will come to you."

"Really?" Adam asked in delight, then stopped and stood regally.

"Give them a name," the Creator prompted.

"Monkeys, come to me," the man said solemnly. The creatures paused from their swinging and obediently scampered down the tree and approached Adam. They peered at him curiously, and then a brave one scampered up his arm and sat on his shoulder—to Adam's delight. The great beasts who had long since gotten over their inhibitions about eating fruit off the tree lumbered over to observe the monkey playing with their prince. The bolder one reached out with his trunk and cautiously touched the man on the back. When Adam spun around in surprise, the beasts stepped back a few paces.

"What a magnificent fellow you are!" the man said. "I will name you—elephant." Then he turned to the Creator. "Why are there two of each?"

"The animals are of two kinds—male and female. This one is the male. The other is the female. Together they will be able to create new young just like them." I could see the tree at the center of the garden that served as the portal to this world shaking with almost visible fury from Lucifer's presence. A wave of understanding flooded over me as I realized yet another reason our ex-leader was so angry. The inhabitants of this planet would probably take reproduction for granted, yet it was something the heavenly inhabitants were not able to do. Lucifer, already furious that the Almighty Ones had not included him in the creation process, now had to watch even the animals They had created for the human prince's enjoyment be able to do something that he had longed to do.

"It just isn't fair," he hissed from the tree. Ignoring him, we turned our attention back to the Creator. He was stroking the elephants' magnificent heads and scratching their trunks.

"Then I will call you he elephant and she elephant," the man announced. The male wrapped his trunk around Adam and lifted him off the ground. "Whoa, he elephant, what are you doing?" the new ruler of this planet shouted, losing all of his dignity as he waved his arms and legs in the air. He elephant placed Adam up on his back. "Oh—ah—thank you," Adam said, regaining his dignity. "This is terrific! Let's go exploring!"

The Creator laughed. "I'll visit you later, Adam," He said. "In the cool of the day, just before the darkness comes, I will come and walk with you every day. And I'll be back then. In the meantime, have fun." He elephant and she elephant lumbered off slowly with Adam, pointing out new things he wanted to see. But it was not the cool of the day yet, and Adam had too many questions to wait.

When he elephant had lifted him down, the man began pacing back and forth with his brow furrowed.

He noticed a brightly colored bird in the branches above him. "You are a pretty fellow," he said. "Come to me." The bird obediently flew down and perched on his left hand. "I don't see anyone else like you," he asked. "Were you created to be alone like me?" The bird tipped its head to one side, looking quizzical. Then we heard a raucous screeching as another bird swooped down and perched on Adam's shoulder. "You don't look alike," he commented. The first bird walked up his arm and began to scratch the other bird's head with its beak and groom its feathers. "Ah," Adam realized, "you would be he parrot and she parrot. And you just look different on the outside because you are not the same as the four-legged beasts." The parrots seemed to nod in agreement.

The human sighed. "I wish I could talk to the Creator. I just don't understand this. All of you—every single animal I have met—has a he beast and a she beast. And yet there is only one of me. The Creator said He would come back in the cool of the evening. But I don't know when that will be. I hope it won't be a very long time." He absentmindedly stroked the back of a large cat who had crept up next to him and was now sitting on its haunches, licking its paws.

"Perhaps if I called," Adam said to himself slowly. "Creator— Creator God." He spoke louder. "Creator God, can You hear me?" It brought a ripple of smiles to all of us who were watching. *Of course He can hear him,* we thought to ourselves.

But the Creator didn't smile. He just stepped up next to Adam and said, "I'm right here with you, Adam. What is it?"

"It's wonderful," the man began. "Everything is wonderful. And yet—well, look at them." The Creator glanced at the animals and nodded. "Uh—well, it's all he beast and she beast, but there is only one of me. I think I'm a he beast."

"You are a man," the Creator said. "Because of that, you are higher than the beasts. But yes, you are a he."

"Do I have a she?" Adam asked sadly.

"No," the Creator replied. "Would you like one?"

The man nodded.

"Very well. It isn't good for man to be alone—it isn't good for any creature to be alone. Therefore, I will create a she human that is part of your very own flesh, and you will treasure her."

"I will," said Adam, glowing with delight. "What part of me are you going to use?"

"Lie down, Adam," the Creator told him, chuckling. "You are going to go to sleep, and I will take just a small piece from your side—you won't miss it at all." Adam looked relieved, as if the Creator would take one of his legs. I think he already realized that the Son of the Almighty was not only very wise but also very practical. Obviously this human still had much to learn. His eyes drifted shut as he missed yet another part of the Creator's magnificent workmanship. My friends and I were grateful that He didn't make us sleep through any of this. We wouldn't have missed it for anything.

SHEENA

he first cry of Sheena delighted me far more than even the birth of baby Cain. For though Cain was the first baby human, Sheena was mine. Those of us whom the Almighty One had assigned recording duties had all been faithfully chronicling the activities of Adam and his wife, Eve. Now as they started to produce children one by one, we received specific assignments, and Sheena was mine. I watched her every choice with delight as she grew—though it was over-shadowed by the knowledge of how much better her life would be had Lucifer not taken over this new world. Trying not to think about the second-greatest grief I had experienced, I concentrated all of my energy on the human child.

"Cain! Cain, wait, I have something to show you," she called as she ran after her older brother.

Turning, he smiled at her. Sheena adored him. She raced down the path carrying a huge basket.

"Here, look at this one," she said. "I just finished it. It's so much better than the last one. Now you can pick your fruit and put it in this. That way you can carry more at a time."

"I liked the last one you made for me," he replied.

The girl wrinkled her nose. "I know you did," she said. "But it was warped on one side. After all, it was the first one I'd ever done."

"It carried fruit."

"Yes—until the handle slipped out and your fruit rolled all over the ground."

They both laughed. "This one is much stronger," she said. "And it's bigger, too. You can carry more."

"Come with me, then. You can help me pick the fruit, and I'll carry it back."

The girl skipped along next to him. "What kind of fruit are we going to get today?"

"You'll love it. They are big and juicy with soft sweet orange flesh on the inside. I call them mangoes."

"They sound wonderful. You are such a good gardener and seem to have something to harvest from the garden for us to eat almost all the time."

"It comes from careful planning," he said. "I spent a long time just learning about the seasons for each of the fruit trees and the other food-bearing plants. The secret is that once you know their seasons and their cycles, you must plant some of each so that there is always something ripening. Then we will always have food for the family."

"You are so smart, Cain. It must take a lot more brains to be a gardener than just to take care of sheep, as Abel does."

He smiled at her. "Yes, sheep have their own problems and they smell funny. But our brother seems to like it, and someone needs to care for them."

Sheena skipped to catch up with him. "I guess so. Still, who'd want to eat a sheep?"

Cain laughed. "Not me. Besides, Abel would get upset if we tried to eat his sheep."

The girl laughed with him. "That's true. He really loves them, and they are useful for their soft wool. Mother is making something for the new baby just today out of some of the wool."

"That and the fact that we have to keep them around so we have something for sacrificing to God."

"Each time we go to the gates of the garden we have to take a perfect lamb and sacrifice it on the altar." Sheena lapsed into thought for a moment. "I hate it when we do that."

Cain glanced at her. "You do?"

"I hate having to kill that poor little lamb."

"It's not the lamb's fault—it's our parents' fault. If they'd just listened to what God said, we'd still be living in the garden, and then Abel wouldn't have to tend sheep. Mother and Father didn't need wool when they lived in there—at least that's what they tell us."

"They didn't wear anything?"

"No," he said, "and they were happy that way. But we have to wear clothes since we have had to live outside the garden."

"H'mm," Sheena said, thinking again.

"If it had been us in there," Cain continued, "you and I would have just done what God said in the first place. I mean, everyone knows snakes can't talk anyway. We would have known something was up. And then we could still live there."

The girl sighed. "I wish they had."

"Well, this basket is about full. Let's head back."

"Supper is going to be great tonight," she said.

And they hurried home.

* * *

"Sheena," Cain called. "Come with me."

"Where are we going?"

"To Eden's gate. It's time for our weekly sacrifice."

Her forehead puckered into a frown. "Where's your lamb?"

"I'm not taking a lamb this time. You'll like this."

He lowered the basket she had made for him. It held some of the most beautiful, most perfect fruit she had ever seen.

"Those are lovely, Cain. Are you going to trade those to Abel for a sheep?"

"No, I am going to offer them to God."

"But—but—"

"I know, we usually give Him sheep. But if I offer Him fruit, then no innocent little lamb has to die for mistakes it hasn't made. I can just offer the best of what I do, and you won't have to see a little lamb die."

"It sounds good," Sheena said cautiously. "But—but it's not what God asked us to do!"

"But He's the Creator, so I'm sure He will appreciate being honored with His handiwork."

"I don't think this is a good idea," the girl protested. But she followed her brother along the trail.

When they arrived at the gate to Eden, Abel was already preparing a lamb on his altar. "What are you doing, Cain?" he said when he saw the basket. "You know God asked us to sacrifice a lamb."

"Mind your own business," his brother snapped.

"But you can't just do things your own way and sacrifice anything you want. God was specific about what He wants us to do. We need to be obedient to Him."

"Mind your own business," Cain repeated, firmly and distinctly enunciating each word.

"It's not what we're supposed to be doing," Abel persisted. "I'm going to tell Father."

Cain turned his back to his brother and continued to arrange his fruit on the altar.

I shook my head. The very son who insisted that he would never have fallen for Lucifer's temptations now considered his opinion equal to that of the Most High. Yet what he was doing was even worse, for the sacrifice of the lamb looked forward to the plan the Almighty and His Son had put into effect. It pointed to the sacrifice of the Son—His life in exchange for that of the humans. The sacrificial lamb symbolized the Son's perfection offered in exchange for their sinful disobedience. In effect Cain was saying that the works of his own hands were just as good as the symbolic perfection of the lamb.

I shuddered! How would the Almighty respond to such blasphemy? With the sacrifice of the lamb, He always showed His acceptance by burning the creature on the altar. Would He strike Cain with fire for his disobedience and disrespect? Breathlessly I watched with the other recorders to see what would happen. The flames from heaven struck Abel's altar and consumed the lamb. Although Cain remained before his altar, nothing happened. As he waited and waited the fire burned out on Abel's altar and the younger brother rose to his feet. Cain stayed on his knees, staring straight ahead.

"I told you," Abel whispered.

Cain's jaw clenched tightly.

Sheena grabbed Abel by the arm. "Stop it, Abel. Go away; leave him alone."

The brother turned and walked up the path. Sheena knelt by Cain for a few minutes, but he ignored her. The anger around him was so real she could almost touch it. Quietly she stood and slowly walked away. *Abel was right,* she thought. *God has asked for a lamb, and obviously He didn't want fruit or He would have honored Cain's sacrifice with fire too.* She shook her head, deciding that Cain's plan had been a bad idea. I shook my head too. Sheena had no idea how terrible Cain's idea was.

"Oh, Cain, there you are," Sheena exclaimed a little later. "I've been looking everywhere for you."

He stood in one of his fields, staring at the ground. For a moment he looked up at her, then back at the ground. She ran over to his side.

"What's the matter? Are you still feeling bad about . . ." Her words stuck in her throat. "Oh, Cain, what happened?"

They both stared at their brother lying on the ground, blood pouring from a wound in his head, soaking into the freshly tilled earth. Numbly she knelt and touched Abel. He didn't move.

"Is he . . . can people die like sheep?" she asked.

Cain nodded. "I think so. At least he's not breathing. I think life has left him."

"Oh, Cain," Sheena whispered, shuddering. "Did you . . . ?"

Her brother looked at her.

"Oh, Cain," she sobbed, throwing her arms around his neck. "What are we going to do?"

He pulled her gently from him. "We aren't going to do anything. You are going to go back home to our parents and keep your mouth shut. I'm going to get out of here."

"Where will you go? You need shelter—you need a family."

"But right now I need to get away before Mother and Father find Abel. Remember how much they grieve over every dead lamb, every dead flower? I don't know if they will be able to bear this."

"Oh, Cain," she whispered. "Come back when it's better. I will miss you." Then she flung her arms around his neck again before running toward home.

I turned to follow her, sensing the presence of the Son. How I wanted to hear what He was going to say to young Cain. However, having been assigned a duty, I followed Sheena.

* * *

Slowly Sheena filled her basket with mangoes from the tree that Cain had planted. It had been several seasons since that horrible day when he had left. She shuddered just thinking about it.

Their parents would probably never get over it. In a way, that day they lost both their sons. For God had banished Cain from the settlement. Squaring her shoulders, she took a deep breath. What God had done was just and fair. The whole family recognized its justice. But she missed Cain. God had told them all that He had put a mark on him to protect him and that no one should try to kill him to avenge Abel's death. It gave her hope, although she wasn't sure that Cain would be able to accept the forgiveness God offered. She wondered if he had built an altar to God wherever he was now and if he ever offered lambs. As she reached for another mango she heard a voice from the tree.

"Sheena."

Startled, she jumped and stepped back. She knew about voices from trees. Mother had told her many times about the serpent and how it had deceived her into disobeying God. Sheena had always marveled at how her mother had eaten the fruit in order to be like God when she already was like God, created in His image. Now the girl stared up into the tree. Had the serpent come back? Was he trying to speak to her?

"Don't look all scared," the voice said. "I'm over here." Then he dropped to the ground.

"Cain," she shrieked, flinging herself into his arms. "Cain, I'm so glad to see you. We didn't know what had happened to you. Nobody's seen you in so long, we didn't know if you were dead or alive." Then she burst into tears.

"I've missed you, too. You were always my best friend. I've been living to the east of here in a land I call Nod. I've built a small settlement. Now I came back to see—well, to talk to you."

"Oh, I'm so glad. I've missed you so much. Are you going to stay?"

"No, I will never live in this settlement again. You know that."

She nodded, brushing her tears away.

"Sheena, I want you to come with me. You are not a little girl anymore. We can start our own settlement and our own home."

The young woman glanced around. "But what about Mother and Father? What about the rest of the family?"

"I guess that's something you'll have to choose," he said. "I can't return here. So if you come with me, I guess you'll be an exile too."

Sheena stared at the ground. "Do you still worship God?"

"In my own way."

She smiled to herself. "Still in your own way?"

Cain stared at the ground. "Yes, I guess I'm still a rebel at heart."

Sheena's guardian edged closer. "No, no," he whispered. "By joining Cain, you'll be a rebel too."

"Think about it," Cain persisted. "If you stay here in the settlement, you will just be Mother and Father's little girl. But if you come with me, you'll be the mother of the new settlement. You'll be queen of the city we're going to build."

What would she do? I could barely look. Yet I couldn't tear myself away.

"Wait here," she said after a few moments. "I'll get my things." Her guardian and I exchanged glances. We both felt ill. This was going to be a painful recording assignment for me, perhaps worse than it had already been.

800 YEARS LATER

The woman approached Eden's gate. Tall and beautiful, she walked with a regal step. Yet there was no spring in it. And she carried a walking stick. Her clothes had been expensive at one time, but were dirty and travel-worn now. White streaked her long hair, her eyes were dull, and her face lined. She stopped in front of the altar by the gate and gazed at the two cherubim still guarding the entrance with their sabers of light. Slowly she knelt before the cold stone altar.

"God of my father, Adam," she whispered. "I bring You nothing. I have no lamb. My husband has died. I have grandchildren and great-grandchildren, yet none of them worship You. I was queen of a grand city with art and industry and civilization and violence and murder and unhappiness. Now I am an old woman and I have left all that. I have come back here to see if You still want me." She paused and swallowed hard. "Is there any coming back? I always felt that You had offered Cain a second chance by not allowing anyone to kill him. I always felt You loved him and cared about him. Do You feel that way about me? Is it too late for me to worship You?"

An old man stepped out of the shadows of the great tree near the gate. "Sheena," he asked, "is that you?"

She turned. "I am Sheena."

He reached out his arms. "I am Seth, your younger brother. You are welcome in my home."

"Seth, you look so different."

For a second he did not know what to say. "Well, so do you," he finally managed.

Shaking with laughter, they fell into each other's arms. "Welcome home, Sheena," he said. "Our parents have both died, but they always hoped you would come back someday. And for now, I will provide you a lamb for a sacrifice."

Someday, I thought to myself, *God will provide the lamb, and*

Sheena will be covered with God's forgiveness, just as her parents have been. The two cherubim at the gate smiled at the brother and sister walking back toward the settlement.

ΠALA

urry up, Nala," her mother called. "We are all ready to go except for you!"

Nala pulled her cloak over her shoulders. "I'm ready now," she said, letting out a deep sigh. She would miss their country home. Moving to the city where her uncle lived would be exciting and new, and Father would work for money instead of farming, but Nala felt so sad inside that she could not work up any excitement. She loved the farm and her animals. Kissing her parrot on the top of his head, she said, "I'll miss you."

He responded by raising his crest and shouting, "Oh, yeah! Oh, yeah!"

"Father, can't I bring Squawker?" she begged.

"Such a pretty boy! Oh, yeah!" the bird yelled.

Father laughed. "Squawker would be miserable in the city. He makes a lot of noise and a lot of mess. They have marble floors in your uncle's house, and his habit of flinging his seed hulls and parts of his dinner everywhere would be a problem, to say nothing of the little 'presents' he leaves. The Nadab family will take good care of Squawker, and he will be much happier here. Now come on, or we'll have to leave you with them too," her father teased.

The heaviness in Nala's chest seemed to grow every mile they went. If leaving her home and her beloved pet wasn't enough, what she overheard her mother and father discussing was even worse. She knew she shouldn't eavesdrop but sometimes a person just couldn't help it—especially when she heard her name come up in their conversation!

"Nala is almost of marriageable age," her father had said. "My brother Hashim has a son who needs a wife. With their family's wealth, Nala would be well provided for and have a much better life than I have been able to give you."

The girl couldn't make out her mother's answer but she had heard enough. Perhaps she should offer a sacrifice and pray to the gods that she wouldn't have to marry her cousin. But she had nothing of value to offer them. A sacrifice had to be valuable to really impress the gods. She thought of Squawker. *I'm so glad I don't have him with me,* she thought fiercely. *I'd rather marry a demon than hurt Squawker. I guess I'll have to cope with this without any divine assistance.*

I smiled. Nala had no idea of the divine assistance that was about to be a part of her life if she just allowed it to happen. I could hardly wait to see how things would unfold, but I knew with her sensitive nature and tender heart that she would have a hard time resisting the love of the Creator if she ever met Him.

* * *

"We're going out today," Kenosh announced from the doorway. "You've been moping around the house for a week. It's time you should get out and have a good time."

"Go ahead without me," Nala answered. "I don't mind spending time alone, and at the moment I don't feel like partying."

"What *do* you feel like doing? How am I supposed to entertain you if you don't even know what you like?"

"I like walking out in the woods by myself. I like animals and birds."

"No woods or animals around here," Kenosh replied. "And women can't go outside the family compound without one of the men with her. It's not safe."

"If there are no animals around here, then how can it not be safe?" Nala puzzled.

"It's not animals—it's the people. Any woman out without a male protector is a free target. Trust me. We have these thick walls and heavy gate for a reason!"

Nala starred at the floor.

"Look," he said patiently, "I'm supposed to take you somewhere and cheer you up. But you've been avoiding me as if I have the breath of a rhinoceros or some evil disease. Is it something I've said or done?"

The girl shook her head.

"I know you're homesick, but this is ridiculous," he continued. "And both our parents are going to get annoyed if we don't at least act like we are having fun. Now tell me what the problem is, and I will make it better. I have the money to spend for whatever it is that your little heart is yearning for, and I am at your disposal all day today."

"It was something I overheard my father say," Nala mumbled.

A look of understanding crossed his face. "So you know of their plans for us."

She nodded, staring hard at her big toe.

"Cheer up! They could have been marrying you off to some stranger. And if I wasn't a family member, you wouldn't even be able to spend time with me or get to know me at all till after the wedding. I know you are very young, but for both our sakes, try to show some interest in life here. I'll tell you what—I'll take you out to Noah's folly. It's out on the edge of town and you can see the hills from there. That thing is huge and the old man is hilarious. There are all sorts of vendors and sideshows that have set up their wares to take advantage of the crowds. You'll love it. Get your cloak."

* * *

Drawing a deep breath, Nala shook her head. "It looks like a huge black palace!" she whispered. "How could anything that size be a boat?"

Kenosh laughed. "I told you he was crazy. It's not shaped right for sailing, because it has no depth to the keel to keep it from tipping over. Anyway, it is too big to drag to any body of water near here. I hear the inside is all open with bars and cages but few actual rooms. I guess that's where they will keep the old man when he gets too crazy to be let out in public."

The noise suddenly increased as an old man climbed to the top of a pile of lumber. "Please! Listen to me!" he pleaded to the vast throng. "The ark is almost finished. The flood could come any day. There is room for anyone who wants to join us. Please choose life! God loves you. That is why He has provided a way for you to escape the approaching disaster."

"Aw, Noah," a heckler shouted from the crowd, "you've been saying that for more than 100 years now. And we're still dry as a bone out here!"

"Even if our river flooded its banks enough to come up and cause damage to the town, there wouldn't be enough water to actually get up this hill and float this monstrosity of yours!" someone else yelled.

"Could that really happen?" Nala asked Kenosh.

"The scientists at the university say that flooding of the scale he has been predicting is impossible," Kenosh replied.

"Please! Listen to me! You are almost out of time," Noah shouted.

"Why are people so mean to him?" Nala whispered.

"Because he's crazy. Because he has been preaching the same

thing for 120 years and nothing has happened. In the beginning some people believed him. Many people here have worked on the ark—he pays well enough even if he is nuts. I hear he is close to bankrupt now, though."

"Kenosh!" a voice in the crowd called to them. "It has been a long time!"

Turning to the man who had spoken, Kenosh started an animated conversation with him. At first Nala listened politely. Soon her mind wandered. She kept thinking about the preacher begging people to accept his invitation into the ark. What would a person do if they did accept his invitation? Go into the ark now? Get a ticket for whenever they thought it was time? What if nothing happened? She edged her way toward the front of the crowd to see a little better.

Soon she was so engrossed in what Noah was saying that she did not realize that she had separated from Kenosh until she turned to ask him a question. "Kenosh? Where are you?" she called.

Suddenly a man grabbed her by the arm. "Come with me, pretty little one," he said.

I looked around. Nala's guardian was already on the spot. He signaled to the guardian behind Noah's son. His guardian leaned down and whispered in Shem's ear. Would the son of Noah be receptive? Would he respond in time?

"No! You're not Kenosh! Help!" Nala screamed.

"I'll be Kenosh or whoever you want me to be," he said with a coarse laugh. "And you'll shut up and come with me."

A tall man jumped down from the platform where Noah stood and approached them. "Do you know this man?" he asked the girl.

"No," she choked out. "Please help me!" The two guardians stood between her and her attacker. The man paled and starred at them in astonishment. I was surprised too. The guardians had materialized though nobody else seemed to notice them except the person trying to abduct Nala.

Anger flashed across his face but he let go of her arm and melted into the crowd. Nala burst into tears. Her human rescuer looked uncomfortable. "Here now," he said. "Stop that. You are safe now. I'm not a threat to young women. Where is your husband? May I take you home?"

"I'm not married," said Nala, trying to stop the tears.

"Oh," he replied. "I'm not either. I'm just used to the city girls around here all being married off so young."

"I'm not from around here," she answered.

"So I gathered. My name is Shem. Would you like to see inside?" He gestured toward the huge ark. "My mother is inside right now, and if we're in luck, she might give us something cool to drink." Nala nodded. "Come this way. The entrance is on the other side."

When she stepped into the shadowed entryway she caught her breath in amazement. She thought from the outside that the ark would be dark and depressing inside. To her surprise, it was open, airy, and light. Openings between the top of the sides and the roofing allowed light to flood into the interior. The center of the ark was like a large atrium with three tiers of decks around the sides. She saw bins of grain and hay, dried fruits, roots and vegetables, and many plants and small trees in pots. Beyond them were what appeared to be cages and stalls. Several different-sized branches attached to the wall resembled the kind of perches that her old pet Squawker would love.

A kind-looking woman approached them. "Shem, whom do you have with you?"

"Um, I'm not sure," he mumbled, now sounding shy.

"Nala—my name is Nala."

"Someone was trying to abduct her out there," Shem explained. "I thought she could use a cool drink and a place to sit for a few minutes."

"Oh you poor thing," the woman said, putting her arm around Nala. "There is so much of that these days. This place is not safe for anyone anymore. No wonder God is angry and wants to destroy it and start over again."

"You believe in that?" the girl blurted in surprise.

"Oh yes. Here, sit down. Shem, you go out and find this girl's family or husband, and I will chat with her while she composes herself."

"My cousin's name is Kenosh," Nala explained. "I was here with him."

"I'll find him," Shem promised, heading for the door.

"Which god is so angry?" Nala asked, returning to the woman's statement.

"The one God. The Creator God. Really the only God. The others are just human-made statues of wood or stone or metal."

Nala nodded. She had often wondered about the gods. Their priests said that they always were mad about something and required expensive sacrifices. "But your God is angry now. Does He require sacrifices too?" the girl questioned.

"Yes, our God is angry right now. But He is angry because His children—like you—are being hurt by others who are so wicked and violent. He loves humans—after all He made us. The Creator designed this earth so we could live peaceful lives caring for the land and our gardens and animals."

Nala nodded. Her life had been that way until recently, even if she hadn't known about the one God. "How do you know for sure that it is true?"

"God told Noah," the woman explained. "I am his wife. We had been married for a long time when it happened. God spoke to him and told him to build this ark and gave him all the directions. Noah was 480 years old. Most people have children by then. We had none. For a while we thought we probably couldn't ever have any. One of the things God told Noah that day was that when the ark was finished, he and I and our sons and their wives would be saved in the ark. But we had no sons!

"Noah started work right away. People laughed when he said our sons would be saved too, when we didn't have any. But 20 years later, I gave birth to Shem."

Nala laughed with delight. "My rescuer!" she exclaimed.

Noah's wife nodded. "And it wasn't long before Ham and Japheth came along too. Sons—just like God said. How can I not believe the rest of the message?"

"How soon do you think the flood is coming?"

"I believe it will be very soon," she replied. "The ark is pretty much finished. I have some more seeds and herbs to move into it and as much fresh stuff as is practical, though we have mostly stored dried foods and things that will last through a long storm. We don't have the animals yet. I'm not sure how Noah intends to take care of that. He doesn't either, but he says God will tell him what to do when the time comes."

"And your sons? Do they believe? And their wives?"

"Our sons will come into the ark when the time comes because God told us they will," she said. "The two youngest are married. Shem is not."

As Shem stepped into the ark and heard the last statement, he colored slightly. "Perhaps that is because I do not care to take as a wife any of these silly little city girls who can't talk of anything but the latest fashions and parties and who are fooling around with someone else's husband," he said defensively. "There are worse things than being single, and I am only 100. That is pretty young considering a person's full life span. You were four times that age when I was born!"

His mother nodded. "I didn't mean to embarrass you, Shem," she said quietly.

"I could not find your cousin, Kenosh," he said, changing the subject. Nala paled.

"It will be all right," Shem's mother comforted. "I'm sure there was a good reason he left."

Shem nodded. "Perhaps there was some emergency or maybe he is looking for you."

"Don't worry; we'll take you home," his mother added.

* * *

Late that night Nala lay on her bed, her blanket stuffed in her mouth to quiet her sobs as she listened to the shouting in the other room.

"How could you have just left? You didn't even find her before you went off for drinks with your friend?"

"I'm a grown man! I have friends and things to do other than babysit some green country girl who doesn't even know how to keep out of trouble! If she wandered off, she deserved whatever she got!"

More shouting.

"Yes, I know I have to marry her because you said so and because your deal with your brother for their land in the country will fall through if I don't. But don't expect me to like it! I'm not one of those 'one god' worshipers. I have many gods and I'll have many wives, and Nala will just have to deal with it like everyone else's wife does!"

Nala crept out of her room and into the next one where her parents were sitting. They had hoped that she wouldn't hear the argument between Kenosh and his father, but she would have been deaf not to.

"We're so sorry!" her mother sobbed.

Her father nodded, swallowing hard. "We were trying to do the best thing for you. We traded the farm so that you could have a good marriage and have the things that we never had."

"He doesn't even want to marry me," the girl blurted out.

"We've already exchanged the property. Kenosh will cooperate because he has to. And so will you."

"I don't want to stay here. And I don't want to get married to Kenosh. I would rather live in Noah's folly than that!"

"Really?" her mother asked incredulously. "Are you a believer in the one God?"

"I think I am," said Nala slowly.

"You know, when I was a little girl I went to Eden's gate with my father. I got to see the angels with the fiery swords. My father said that the one God lived in there and that He had the angels guarding the gate and that no humans except my uncle had ever been in there."

"Your uncle?" asked Nala.

"Yes, Uncle Enoch was a one God worshiper. They say he walked with God all the time. Not that he could see Him, but he talked to God about everything and apparently God talked to him too. Uncle Enoch talked about this flood thing like Noah does."

"So you believe in this?" her father asked, staring at her mother as if seeing her for the first time.

"No, well, maybe . . . well, I don't know. I never met Uncle Enoch but they say he never died. When we went to Eden's gate that time I kept peering in past the angels, hoping I could see him but I never did. But they say he never died and that God took him to live with Him. They say you live forever if you get into the garden and eat from that tree of life. I'll bet he's still there."

"Please help me to get back to Noah's ark," Nala interrupted. "His mother told me that they are moving into it. She thinks things will be over very soon now."

"Well, I don't know about that," the girl's father commented. Nala's guardian leaned over and whispered to him. The man's face creased with worry.

"Let's help her," his wife exclaimed. "This isn't anything like we planned. Perhaps she will be happier living with the God worshipers. At least she will be treated kindly."

"My brother will kill me!" he grumbled as he pulled on his cloak. "Let's hope the God worshipers are still awake."

By morning, the arrangements had been made. It was a bitter-sweet parting. I had hoped Nala's parents would stay and join the ark party too. It was a difficult decision for them but the dark side let out a loud cheer as they tearfully kissed Nala and turned back to the city before daylight. Nala cried. Noah's wife held her and sobbed too. Noah raised his hand in blessing. "Don't be afraid," he said. "Our family and our God will protect Nala and care for her all the days of her life. The girl will be blessed and fulfilled. She has made a wise choice. Your love for her will always be remembered. Thank you for bringing her to us." Then he turned and walked back into the ark. The rest of his family and Nala followed.

"We must find you a husband among the worshipers of the one God. Then you will be protected if your cousin Kenosh returns to claim you and take you away."

"Can he do that?" Nala asked fearfully.

"Legally, yes," Noah replied. "But God is the protector of all in this family. He will not allow anything to happen that He has not provided for."

"But who would want to marry me?" Nala said. "What Kenosh said is true. I am only a little country girl who doesn't know how to stay out of trouble."

"I would," said a voice from the shadows. Shem stepped forward. "I have waited for a woman who would be willing to turn her back on the city and live as God intended for us. One who would care more for a godly life than wealth and parties. One who would choose God above anything else. I would marry you, Nala, but only if you will have me."

She turned toward him. "Yes, I will have you."

"Father, can we be married now?"

"Yes, I would feel safer to have things settled before Nala's relatives show up," his father said. Noah sacrificed a lamb on the family altar and then lifted his hands in blessing and bound the two together for life. Nala became the only wife of Shem, son of Noah, worshiper of the one God.

Before any of them had a chance to savor the moment, a rumbling reached their ears. "Quick, grab what you have left to take aboard and get into the ark!" Noah shouted.

"Is it the flood?" Nala asked.

"I don't know," Shem responded. "Let's just go. We'll know soon."

The family rushed up the ramp and into the open ark as the sun crept up over the distant hills. As the light flooded the valley below the ark they caught their breath in amazement. Hundreds—no thousands—of animals all walked in an orderly manner straight for them.

"Quick, my sons!" Noah directed. "Open all the doors to all the cages and stalls."

"How will we know where to put which ones?" Ham questioned.

"They are all coming at once!" Japheth exclaimed.

Nobody had any answers—they just raced through the ark, flinging open each door. The animals did not pause but marched straight up the ramp and into the boat. It was not all that surprising to me, since I could see the guardians leading each pair or group of seven (if they were clean animals) up the ramp and into their stalls, but I'll admit that it would have looked a little spooky to me too if I couldn't have seen what was guiding them.

Now Noah and his sons walked up and down the aisles, closing each door and gate and speaking quietly to the beasts and birds. Even the insects went straight to Mrs. Noah's plants and settled in, some starting their nesting and egg-laying immediately.

Nala stared in astonishment. If there had been any doubt in her mind about the one God, the events of the past hour had totally erased it. She picked up some bread and offered some crumbs to the tiny birds perched nearest to her. They pecked at it gratefully. Tears welled up in her eyes as she thought of Squawker. "Oh, one God," she whispered. "I know You have done so much today already. You rescued me from all my problems and gave me a husband, too. I just have one more thing to ask. Please put parrots on the boat before we leave. I miss Squawker so much. I . . ."

A flapping of wings interrupted her prayer. A pair of bright green parrots with yellow heads swooped in and landed on the perch near the door. Nala shrieked in delight. "The one God has listened to me!"

"Oh, yeah! Oh, yeah" screamed the little male as he flapped down to Nala's shoulder.

"Squawker! Is it really you?"

"Oh, yeah! Oh, yeah!" the parrot yelled. "Such a pretty boy!"

"I love you, one God!" Nala cried.

"Oh, yeah!" Squawker screamed.

Terah

 shmael jumped up onto an outcropping of rock and shouted, "I am Ishmael, king of the desert and feared by all other desert kings."

Terah bowed low before him. "Hail, King of the Desert," the 10-year-old proclaimed. He looked up just in time to see Ishmael's pet goat charging behind him. "Look out," he yelled, but his warning was too late and the future king of the desert fell onto his royal rear. Terah shook with laughter. "Now, Belzer," he scolded, "that's hardly the way to treat the future king of the desert."

Ishmael stood, brushing the dust from his cloak. "Belzer is just like Sarah," he complained. "She doesn't think how her actions might cause her problems later when I am the king of this camp."

I glanced around, hoping that his voice could not carry across the dry desert air to Sarah's tent, not far away. Ishmael continued, "You should just see how she treats my mother. When I am ruler of this camp, my mother will be the head of the household. And when that happens, Sarah will have to treat her with greater respect." I nodded. Everyone was loyal to Abraham, Ishmael's father. And while he and his wife, Sarah, were devoted to each other, she could be occasionally difficult to get along with. Tension and even anger had flared between her and Hagar, Ishmael's mother, as long as Terah could remember.

"When that time comes," Ishmael continued, "I am going to make it up to my mother for all the insults and indignities she's had to suffer from my father's wife over these years. You would think that Sarah would have the foresight to think of that and consider what her future will be like once my father is gone."

The words made Terah squirm. "Anyway, maybe Sarah thinks she will die first and not have to deal with it, " he suggested.

With a sigh Ishmael nodded, then turned to his goat who was preparing for a second charge. "Hey, Belzer, come here. I'll show you who is boss!" And he raced toward the animal and wrestled him to the ground. Straddling the squirming animal, he shouted, "Now, who is the boss here? Do you admit defeat and declare your allegiance to the desert king, Ishmael?" The goat grunted in submission and the 13-year-old rolled off and let him get up.

Suddenly Terah stopped laughing. "Look," he said. In the distance three travelers shimmered in the hot desert air.

"Looks like we are going to have guests," Ishmael said. "We'd better let father know. They will reach here about mealtime."

"Good idea," his friend replied. "That way the women can prepare for three extra people."

Ishmael laughed. "There's always enough food for three extra people. My father provides well for this camp. No one ever goes hungry."

Terah nodded. It was true. Abraham was the wealthiest sheik in the desert, and he did provide well for his clan.

The boys hurried back toward the camp. But Abraham could already see the visitors and left his tent to greet them. They followed him back to his tent. "I wonder if they're dignitaries," Ishmael mused.

Terah shrugged. "Who knows?"

"Let's go find out." They walked slowly by the back of the tent, close enough that they could hear what was being said, but they kept moving so that if anyone saw them they could insist that they were just passing by.

"A son?" they heard Abraham say. "I wish that You could just accept Ishmael as my heir. He could worship You and lead my people." The young man flashed a huge smile at Terah and walked a little taller.

"No," said the other voice. "Your heir will come from Sarah. She will bear you a son."

Ishmael's face clouded. Then they heard Sarah's bitter laugh on the other side of the curtain. Terah raised his eyebrows. Apparently they weren't the only ones eavesdropping.

"Let's get out of here," he whispered. He and Ishmael ran back to a nearby ravine where they could privately discuss what they had heard.

"Who are these strangers?" Terah asked.

"Maybe it's the Nameless One," Ishmael whispered.

"Abraham's God? Coming to visit him in person?"

"It's possible."

"Doesn't He usually speak to Abraham in visions or dreams or a voice in the night?" Terah protested.

Ishmael nodded. "Yes, but He *did* come in person to my mother."

His friend had forgotten that incident.

"She's told me about it many times. Sarah was so mean to her when she was expecting me. After she had her beaten mercilessly, my mother ran away into the desert. The Nameless One came to her and told her she was going to give birth to a son who would lead a nation that would be great. That's why she came back. No point in dying in the desert when you could be the mother of a desert king. Even if she did have to put up with Sarah for a few years."

"Yes, I do remember now. So why would the same God who told your mother to return and made that promise to her also be promising Abraham a different heir?"

Ishmael slumped onto a rock. "I don't know. Could He have forgotten His promise?" Abraham insisted that the Nameless One never changed, he reminded himself, never backed out on any promises. So what could be happening? Both boys were stumped. Ishmael sat with shoulders drooping, his chin in his hands. "I just don't understand," he said. Terah dug in the dirt with his toe. It didn't make sense to him, either. They sat for a while in silence, and then slowly headed back toward camp.

By that evening the visitors had left in the direction of Sodom. "They were probably going to see Lot, my cousin." Ishmael guessed.

Terah nodded. As far as they knew, Lot and his family were the only other believers in the Nameless One who lived in that direction. Everyone else in Sodom worshiped idols. The city was noted for its immorality.

The boy secretly wondered if Lot ever felt sorry he had taken his family there. Rumors kept filtering back about bad behavior among Lot's servants.

"Maybe the Nameless One is going to go straighten him out," Ishmael suggested. Both boys laughed.

A few minutes later Abraham's chief steward and Terah's grandfather, Eliezer, emerged from one of the tents. "Come on, you two,

SURVIVORS OF THE DARK REBELLION

there's work to be done. We're leaving in the morning."

"Where are we going?" Terah asked.

Eliezer shrugged. "South, Terah. South."

"Do you know how far south?" Ishmael questioned.

The servant shook his head. "No, we don't. But the Lord is going to be destroying Sodom, and we would like to be as far out of the way as possible when that happens."

"We are pretty far," Terah said.

"Well, Abraham wants to be farther away. So we need to pack up and get ready. We'll be leaving long before dawn."

Ishmael and Terah had helped move camp many times before and had it down to a science. Although it contained more than 1,000 people, it was very organized. And they knew exactly what to do. Secretly Terah thought it was good for Ishmael to have heavy work to do to keep his mind off what they had heard in the tent. But it still bothered him.

The journey south was long, hot, and dusty. "If we have to get this far away," Ishmael said after a long silence, "what's going to happen to Lot, so close to where God is going to destroy the city?"

"I don't know," Terah answered. "Maybe God told him to go far away too. I'm sure the Nameless One wouldn't just leave him there to perish with it."

Ishmael shrugged. "I don't know. Lot doesn't always think things through carefully. Remember how he treated Father when we were dividing up grazing rights?"

"Yes, I've heard that he was pretty selfish—and foolish. But still he worships the same God. And we did see the visitors heading his way after they talked to your father."

"Well, wherever Lot went for shelter, it wasn't this way, because we haven't seen anyone following us."

Terah said nothing. Lot's family and servants seemed pretty happy in Sodom. They had settled in and become part of the community. He wondered if it would be difficult to convince them to flee as Abraham's camp had. And residing in a house made it much more difficult than living in portable tents.

They had been waiting several hours for Abraham to negotiate permission for them to make camp in the area. Because somebody always owned the good land, one could not just pitch camp or graze anywhere. Finally Abraham returned and ordered everybody to set up camp. They were between the cities of Kadesh and Sur and needed a large empty space for a clan their size.

Abraham had been visiting with the king of the nearest small town, Gerar, and came back in a good mood. It appeared that he and King Abimelech were going to be good friends. A group would spend the rest of the evening pitching their tents and making their camp while Abraham, Sarah, and Eliezer, Terah's grandfather, attended a feast put on by King Abimelech in their honor.

"As the mother of his heir, Abraham should really be taking my mother to the feast," Ishmael muttered.

Hagar came around the corner of a tent just as he said it and overheard his mumbling. "Hush, Ishmael," she said. "You may be right, but you shouldn't say it out loud. That will only get me in more trouble."

He laughed. "Oh, Mother, the things you have said to Sarah have gotten you into more trouble than anything I've said."

She sighed. "Someday it will be different."

The discussion bothered Terah. Seeing his reaction, Ishmael teased him. "Don't be so afraid. The only reason what we're saying makes you uncomfortable is that you've been a servant and a son of a servant and a grandson of a servant all your life. So you haven't tried to imagine anything different. But you're named after my grandfather, who was willing to leave his home and try something different. You need to be more adventuresome and be willing to change. As for me, I'm not going to live this way forever. In fact, I don't like living this way now."

Terah supposed that was true, but it still seemed disloyal to speak with such anticipation about one's father's death. The boy couldn't imagine losing his own father. It would be terrible. Just the idea of it made a knot grow in his stomach. *Perhaps we servants are different,* he thought. *But Hagar has always been a servant and a slave.* Shaking his head, he decided that he wouldn't try to figure it out right now. He had work to do.

* * *

"Wake up! Wake up!"

Terah rolled over. "What's the matter?" he mumbled.

"I have to talk to you!" Ishmael said.

Slowly Terah stumbled along behind him far enough from camp to where they could whisper without being overheard. "It's all coming true the way God promised," Ishmael blurted.

"What, is Sarah pregnant?" Terah asked uneasily.

"No, no! I mean, the way it's supposed to be. Sarah's gone."

"Gone?"

"Yes. The other night when they went to that feast with King Abimelech—well, you know that even though Sarah is 90, men still find her attractive."

Terah shrugged. "I suppose, although servants are not allowed to look at her. And she wears those heavy veils all the time. But her eyes are beautiful."

"Yes, yes," Ishmael said impatiently. "Well, King Abimelech asked Abraham who she was, and Abraham told him Sarah was his sister."

The servant boy looked puzzled. "Why would he do that?"

"Because he was scared. What if King Abimelech tried to kill him to get her? I've heard he did the same thing when he was in Egypt."

"Well, if he knew that Sarah is Abraham's wife, wouldn't he have hesitated?"

Ishmael laughed. "He might have, but since he thinks Sarah is

Abraham's sister, he sent his men this evening. They took her away to be Abimelech's bride—straight to the harem. She's gone!"

Terah blinked and swallowed several times.

"Do you realize what this means? It means my mother is the number one woman in the camp. And I'm finally going to have my rightful place without any of Sarah's interference."

His friend remained silent for a moment, then asked, "But what about God's promise to Abraham that an heir would come through Sarah?"

"Well, I guess God can't do that now."

"You know the Nameless One can hear you even out here," Terah whispered. "He's the God of the desert, too."

"I don't think He hears much. If He had, He would have helped my mother a long time ago. But isn't this wonderful?"

Reluctantly Terah nodded, his feelings a confused jumble inside him. Was this really God's solution to all their problems? What about His covenant with Abraham? And His promise to Sarah? As he lay back down on his pallet to sleep a few minutes later, everything swirled around in his mind. What had just happened didn't fit with the other things he had been taught about the God of Abraham. This wasn't how He worked. What was wrong? Could the God of Abraham be trusted? He dropped into a restless sleep filled with nightmares about the family he served. By the time morning arrived he was exhausted.

* * *

Stripping the last piece of bark off of the twig he had been whittling, Terah clamped it between his teeth. Ishmael continued to throw stones at the large rock in front of them. "I don't understand," he kept saying. "Sarah's been gone a while now. Why is Abraham leaving everything the way it is?"

"They have always been very devoted to each other," Terah observed.

Ishmael spun around. "What does that matter? She's gone now! He wasn't devoted enough to tell the king he was married to her. My mother should be in the first woman's tent. Instead, it stands empty as if Abraham somehow expects Sarah back someday."

The servant boy glanced back toward camp. It was true. Sarah's tent stood just as it had that first day. Abraham had left all of her belongings exactly as they were. And he was moping around in as bad a mood as Ishmael.

Suddenly Terah's teeth clamped down on the twig, cracking it with force. "Ishmael," he hissed, "look over there." The adrenaline poured through both boys' bodies as they stared at Abimelech and his entire force of men marching swiftly toward them. The two raced as fast as they could back to camp.

As quickly as possible all of Abraham's men joined him as they walked out to meet Abimelech. When they came within speaking distance of each other, Abraham called out, "Abimelech, my brother-in-law, what does this mean?"

"Abraham," the king shouted back, "how could you do this to me? How could you bring such a sin on my family? How could you even think of causing the death of an entire tribe? Do you hate us so that you would do this to us?"

"I don't understand," Abraham stammered. "What great sin?"

Terah glanced over at his grandfather who met his eyes and than looked at the ground. What great sin? They could think of one. Still they remained silent. It was not a servant's place to even consider such things, no matter how obvious they were.

"Your wife!" Abimelech hissed.

"Wife?" Abraham replied, trying to sound surprised.

"Don't play games with me," the king snapped. "Your God came to me in the night and told me I would die because I have taken your wife. None of our women have been able to bear children since I took Sarah. I told your God that I had no idea she was your wife and that you had told me she was your sister. Why would you lie to me like that?"

"Well, I wasn't really lying." Abraham protested lamely. "She and I are from the same father. We had different mothers, so she is my sister—but yes, she is also my wife."

"Why didn't you say so?" the king shouted. "I wouldn't have taken your wife from you."

Abraham hung his head in embarrassment and shame. "I was afraid. I was afraid that you would find her as beautiful as I do and kill me and take her."

Abimelech snorted in anger. "So what if I did? You would have lost her either way. And you're just assuming that I'm that kind of person. Well, I'm not!

"We were good people before you came. And if your God lets us live, we will continue to be. Here is your wife." He forced Sarah forward. "She has not been touched. I've also brought you some sheep and some cattle. I want you to sacrifice some of them to your God and ask Him to please remove His curse from us, because we didn't know what we were doing. I would not have taken your wife if I had known who she was."

Abraham nodded. "I will. I will explain everything to the Lord, and I'm sure He will remove His curse because you are innocent."

"Well, you go ahead and do your explaining. Your God—He seems already to know what is going on. I just don't want my people to suffer any more because of your cowardice and dishonesty." Turning on his heel, he left, the crowd of men following him.

Abraham turned and looked as his people. By now the whole encampment had gathered, straining to hear everything. It wasn't difficult. Abimelech's angry voice carried well. "Come," Abraham said, "let's make a sacrifice to God. You have all heard this, and now you all will witness my sacrifice and my confession of my sin. The Lord is merciful, and He will forgive me." To the heavily veiled

Sarah standing in front of him, he said, "And you, Sarah, will you forgive me?"

Sarah was silent for a moment and then reached her hand out toward her humbled husband. He clasped it in his and they slowly walked to the center of the camp where the altar of worship stood. Terah looked at Ishmael who had balled his hands into tight fists at his sides. Tears filled the young man's eyes. Was he that moved to see Sarah back?

"It's not fair," Ishmael hissed. "It's not fair. It's just not fair. This isn't how it was supposed to happen."

"Come, my son," Abraham said to him, "you must stand at my side for the sacrifices."

Ishmael closed his eyes for a moment, and when he opened them again the traces of emotion were gone. "Yes, Father," he said in a flat voice. And he followed Abraham into the camp.

* * *

I watched Terah sleeping quietly. It seemed many years since all that had happened to him. But it was just a blink of an eye to me. Now Terah was a young man. Still honest and devoted to Abraham, his desert king, as his father and father's father were.

It had been a hard choice. With the spring rains after the encounter with Abimelech, God had healed the king's tribe, their women began bearing children again—and so did Sarah. The disappointment and anger that Ishmael had experienced had torn Terah. Ishmael was his best friend, but Abraham was his master. Some days he didn't know what to think.

Ishmael kept his hatred hidden behind a perilous façade that he hardly ever let slip. However his teasing of baby Isaac had a bitterness to it, and it left Terah very uncomfortable. It made Sarah livid and she drove Hagar and her son out of the camp. Abraham was heart-broken and everyone in the camp heard his sobs the day the patriarch said goodbye to his firstborn son. Yet it seemed the only way to bring peace. The Lord had told him to go ahead and send them away, and that He would take care of them. But it broke Abraham's heart.

Until Isaac had been born he had always considered Ishmael his heir, and it seemed heartless to send the boy and his mother alone out into the desert. How would they survive? Was the Lord really keeping His promise or was He merely getting rid of a problem? What Abraham may have lacked in faith, though, he made up for in obedience. And the Lord did take care of Ishmael and Hagar. After all, Ishmael was Abraham's seed—just as young Isaac was.

As time passed, reports returned to the camp of his desert adventures. And he was developing a large family and following like his father's.

Meanwhile Isaac grew into a young man. Having reached the end of his teen years, he was even growing a little beard, although it was thin and patchy on the side. After Ishmael's departure, Abraham had appointed Terah as Isaac's servant. Terah had protected him, played with him, and watched over him loyally from that day on.

Abraham's heavy tread came closer and closer to Terah's tent. The old man had finished crying. He had wiped his face, but his eyes were still puffy. Perhaps to the human eye it might look as if he had just been awake all night praying—which was true.

"Terah," he said, "wake up."

The servant sprang to his feet. "What's the matter? Are we being attacked? Where's Isaac? Is there a problem?"

"No—no problem. Isaac and I are going to make a journey to make a sacrifice. We would like you to come with us. Bring a few other servants to carry wood and provisions. It's about a three-day walk from here."

"I will get things together right away. I can be ready in an hour."

"Good. I'd like to leave before sunrise."

As Terah led the two sleepy servants and the donkey loaded with provisions toward Abraham's tent, Abraham stepped out with Isaac. They whispered to each other, and the tent had no lamps lit, just the coals from the fire of the night before.

"Aren't you going to say goodbye to Mother?" Isaac said quietly.

"No, let her sleep. She's very tired. I've left a message with Eliezer for her, telling her where we've gone. Let's just go."

Terah looked at Isaac. Their eyes met, and Terah shrugged.

It was a rugged journey. We left the grazing land and hiked over steep and rocky terrain. Terah and Isaac, who always enjoyed each other's company, were having a great time chatting about the journey and joking with the servants. Abraham seemed to be in another world, musing on things he cared not to say, only responding when asked a question.

On the third day we came to a valley surrounded by several hills. Above one of the mountain's ridges, toward the end, hovered a cloud. The servants stared at it uncomfortably.

"Yes," Abraham said, "it is the presence of the Lord. That is where we are going." He stopped at the base of the hill. "Terah, you and the servants stay here. Isaac will carry the wood, and he and I will ascend the mountain alone." Abraham took the clay pot with the live coals in it.

"But Father," Isaac asked, "what are we going to sacrifice? Where's the lamb?"

Abraham turned slowly and looked at his son. His eyes filled with tears and he shifted his gaze to the ground. "The Lord will provide a lamb."

Isaac shrugged. God had told his father things before that hadn't made sense to people at the time. Perhaps this was just another example.

Terah tied a rope around the wood so it would be easier for Isaac to sling it onto his back, and the father and son started to climb.

"Come on," Terah told the other servants, "let's set up camp here. Since we're obviously going to be here a while, we may as well get comfortable. I have some dried lentils. Spread out and see what you can find to put in our cooking pot to make this lentil stew worth eating."

I watched closely, doing my duty of protecting Terah. But I wanted to be up on Mount Moriah with Abraham. I had heard his conversation with God during the night before they left, as everyone slept. The Lord had told him to bring Isaac to this mountain and sacrifice him.

I couldn't understand why the Mighty One wanted a human sacrifice. We had watched carefully as He outlined the plan of salvation and knew that someday His Son would come and be sacrificed as a human for the sins of the planet. But was Isaac really the promised one? Had we missed it somehow? Surely not. Then what was God doing? Only the pagans practiced human sacrifice. God's people sacrificed lambs in expectation of the Lamb that God would someday provide for their sins.

I studied Terah. He was obviously as perplexed as I was. Yet he kept the other servants busy, setting up tents and preparing dinner, to ignore the concerns he felt.

Terah stared at the impenetrable cloud that covered the mountaintop and wished he knew what was going on. He had a terrible feeling in the pit of his stomach that he did know, and he tried to shrug it off, but couldn't. He had seen other people make sacrifices to their gods when they brought only the wood and a young person to the altar. Followers of the Nameless One abhorred the custom. They did not practice human sacrifice, and yet it appeared that was what Abraham's God was requiring of him. Surely he had proved his loyalty time and time again. The God of Abraham had taken one son from him, and now was asking him to sacrifice the other.

Thoughtfully Terah rubbed his temples. He had lived many years in Abraham's camp, and it seemed as if every time they had faced danger God had delivered them, had kept His promises. But now— it made no sense. Surely Abraham's God would not make him kill his son. Could it be that after all this, Ishmael would be the only heir?

Terah frowned. That had never seemed to be God's plan—just Hagar and Abraham's. The mountain was not a high one. Suddenly a stomach-wrenching cry from an old man shattered the stillness and echoed from the surrounding hills. "My God," he cried, "I do this thing out of loyalty to You."

Than Terah heard another muffled shout, and then sobs. Thunder reverberated in the distance. *Surely not,* he thought. *Oh, please, God of Abraham, surely he hasn't done it! How could he do this? How could You require this? Do You even know what heartbreak it is for him to lose the only son he has left?* Tough desert man that he was, Terah put his head on his knees and wept.

While they waited for Abraham to return to the foot of the mountain, the servants busied themselves with breaking down the camp, feeding the donkey, and packing their few supplies on its back for the return journey.

Only an hour or two later they heard footsteps coming down the mountain but still within the cloud. Suddenly, as the mist parted, Terah gave a shout. "Isaac!" He flung himself on the young man. They hugged each other unashamedly as Abraham began to sob again. The other two servants busied themselves with the donkey, pretending they were miles away.

Isaac and Terah hugged each other and laughed. "It's good to see you. You were up there for ages," Terah said.

"My father's God is awesome," Isaac observed. "He did provide a lamb. It was right there tangled up in the thicket. We just didn't see it until . . . until . . ."

"Until the lord planned for us to see it," Abraham suggested.

"Yes," Isaac agreed.

"So this trip involved what I feared until you saw the lamb?" Terah asked.

Abraham met his eyes for the first time in the entire trip. "What a terrible thing to have to sacrifice," the old man said slowly.

"Your only son now that Ishmael is gone."

"My laughter," Abraham replied, making a play on the meaning of Isaac's name.

Terah nodded. "We heard you."

"Ah, did you hear the answer?"

"No," Terah replied, "just thunder."

"It was the Lord!" Isaac said. "Father shouted, 'Out of loyalty to You I give my son,' and God answered, 'No, don't kill the lad. Out of loyalty to you, I will give My Son.'"

Abraham smiled although beneath his heavy beard his chin was quivering. "It's the lamb," he said. "We sacrificed the lamb, looking forward to Him giving His son to save us. I never understood what overwhelming love and loyalty it would take to give your son to save someone. I almost couldn't do it. How very much He must love us."

Terah swallowed hard. He thought of his son, now a 2-year-old toddling about the camp. Could he have offered him to the God of Abraham if he had been asked? Shuddering, he closed his eyes, thankful that the God of Abraham had not tested him in that way. "How much He must love us," the servant agreed.

I had watched these humans sacrificing lambs since Eden, and yet the meaning of it just now pierced through not only my intellectual understanding but my feelings too. Abraham's grief on the mountain was heart-wrenching, and yet his love for Isaac was so small compared to the Almighty's love and bond with His Son. Yes, truly, how much the Mighty One loved these humans. All of them. So much that it may take them an eternity to understand.

Asenath

senath put her arms up as Senetenpu, her maidservant, pulled the sheer white linen dress over her head and slipped it into place. "A perfect fit," the woman said. "Lady Asenath, you look beautiful."

The girl twirled around. Now that she was a young lady, she could dress like other women. It also meant she could attend some of the official events with her father.

"Hold still," her maid admonished as she slipped the large wig onto Asenath's head. Until now, Asenath's head had been shaved, except for one lock of hair on the side like all other Egyptian children. But now that she was a woman she would wear the thick black wigs with gold ornaments. "This one is beautiful, but let's try this other one."

Asenath looked at her reflection in the polished brass mirror. The wigs made her head look so big, but they also made her feel much taller. She twirled around again. "What do you think?" she asked Senetenpu.

"It looks very nice. Now try this one." It took several tries to choose the one she liked the best. "Now for your makeup," the maid continued. "Sit still and close your eyes. No! Don't squeeze your eyelids together so tightly when I touch them."

"But it feels weird." Asenath protested.

"Well, it does in the beginning," the woman laughed, "but you get used to it. I will be putting on your makeup until you learn to do it yourself, but you need to practice. No Egyptian woman would be caught outside without her eyeliner on."

Asenath nodded.

"No! Don't nod your head either." She wiped the black smudge off the girl's forehead. "You need to hold perfectly still while I'm doing this."

"I'm sorry, I forgot," Asenath said. "I guess there's a lot more to being a woman than I expected. It will take me a little while to get it all right."

Senetenpu laughed. "Take your time—you have plenty of it. After all, you're very young."

"I'm not that young," Asenath retorted. "I'm 12 years old."

"Yes, you are. Your mother would have been so proud of you if she had lived." The conversation fell silent after that. Asenath didn't remember her mother. In her mind it had always been just her and Father and her maidservant, who had raised her since she was a baby.

"Put these bracelets on," Senetenpu continued. "Now walk across the room, and let's see how you do. Keep your shoulders up and your head held high. Remember, you are the daughter of the high priest of On. You are the first lady of one of the most royal families in Egypt, except for Pharaoh himself. Always remember that when you are in public, and walk with great dignity. No jumping and climbing trees unless you are alone or with your father, or here at home."

Asenath wrinkled her nose. "That's a lot to remember."

"Yes, but it will soon come naturally to you if you practice."

"I am so glad that father is taking me with him today. We are going to a big feast at Potiphar's house in Avaris."

The servant woman nodded. "Remember, he is the captain of the king's guard and all of the security for the palace. His family is extremely wealthy and very important."

"What is it going to be like, Senetenpu?"

"You will love Potiphar's house. I was there once before you were born, when I was tending your mother. It's a beautiful house with huge pillars and beautiful wall paintings, fountains, and gardens."

"Will there be anybody there for me to talk to? Are there girls my age?"

"I don't know. It depends who else has been invited to the feast. Pharaoh does not have children your age. Nor do Potiphar, the captain of the guard, and his wife. They have boys and they're much younger than you are, so they probably won't be at the feast. But you will have a good time. Remember, you are a woman now, so you can converse with adults. Besides, Potiphar's wife is much younger than he is. You may like her."

"I hope so," Asenath said. "This is all so new and exiting, but it would be easier if I had a friend."

It seemed like forever until her father finished in the temple, washing and dressing the god Ra and giving him his flowers and breakfast gifts of the day. Then he assigned duties to the other priests who would be caring for the temple while he was away, and headed for his barge docked on the Nile.

Asenath and Senetenpu were already aboard, and the girl was eager to leave. "Father!" she cried as she rushed to meet him. "I thought you would never get here."

Her father stopped and just stared at her, speechless.

"What's the matter? Do you like it?" She twirled round and round. The bracelets on her arms tinkled.

"You are beautiful, Asenath." He seemed to be having a hard time talking.

"Do you like this wig? Because if you don't, Senetenpu and I brought the other two along. It was hard to pick out which one was my favorite, but I think I like this one with all the little gold jewels on the ends of all of the braids. Isn't it lovely?"

Her father swallowed hard. "In that dress and your wig, you looked so much like your mother that it took my breath away."

His daughter smiled shyly. "I'm so glad, because everyone says my mother was a beautiful woman."

"Well, enough of this. Let's take my beautiful woman up to Avaris."

The sun was low in the sky and the Nile reflected all the beautiful colors of sunset as the barge floated up to the dock at Avaris. Her father helped Asenath step onto the dock, and they walked together to meet Potiphar, chief of Pharaoh's guard. The palace official had a younger man with him. The two bowed.

"Life, prosperity, and health, priest of On," Potiphar said in the traditional greeting.

"Life, prosperity, and health, captain of the guard."

They smiled. Their greetings were formal, but they were friends.

"This is Joseph, as you know, manager of my estates." The slave bowed.

"This is Asenath, my daughter," the priest said. His daughter bowed also, feeling self-conscious in her heavy wig.

"I have my chariots here, and I have a chariot for you," Potiphar said. "Joseph, will you bring Asenath along? The servants will escort the rest of your belongings and entourage to the house later."

The two men strode off, talking quietly about the upcoming festivities.

Joseph looked at Asenath. "Would you prefer to ride in a chariot or one of the wagons?"

"Oh, please take me in a chariot! That way we can keep up with Father."

He laughed. "Even if we do, we must ride behind them. That is the proper etiquette."

The girl laughed with delight. "You're right. Father loves to be in the fastest chariot. Even if our horses are faster, we should probably pretend that they're not."

Joseph helped her up into the chariot. "Here, you stand in front of me and hang on." Then he tapped the backs of the horses with the reins and they started on their way.

Asenath forgot she was now a young woman and squealed with delight. She felt as if she was flying, having never gone so fast. She threw her head back and drank in the pleasure of the ride. Soon they arrived at Potiphar's home and slowed to a stop behind her father and the captain of the guard.

She turned to Joseph. "Thank you."

Looking down at her, he said, "Here, just a minute." Then he straightened her wig, which had been blown slightly off the back of her head and to the side.

Her face flushed red with embarrassment. "I forgot all about that. I haven't been wearing one very long, and I forget it's there."

Joseph laughed. "It looks very becoming on you, and you'll be just fine. Just don't go on too many chariot rides without hanging onto it."

"I doubt that I'll get to go on very many. Father says chariots are not for women."

"Then you probably won't, but there are many other exciting things you'll get to do. So don't worry too much about chariots."

Smiling gratefully at him, she stepped to the ground. Her father and Potiphar were still deep in conversation. She walked slowly behind them through the ornate gardens. "This is beautiful," she said to Joseph who continued to accompany her.

"Yes, Potiphar's gardens are some of the most lovely in all of Egypt."

Asenath wandered off the walkway to look in the lily ponds. "Look, Heket, the frog goddess, has come out and is sitting on her lily pad."

"These ponds were made for the frogs."

The girl laughed. "She doesn't look very divine—just a happy little green creature grateful for the sun." Suddenly she whispered, "I don't really believe in the frog goddess. I don't think she has any power at all."

"Neither do I," he whispered back, "but don't tell anybody. That's not a popular way to think here in Avaris."

The girl drew herself to her full height. "Anyone should know that the sun god is much more powerful than the frog god, anyway. Look at her—I believe she's worshiping the sun."

"She's not going to do it much longer if you get any closer," he said. Then the frog leaped off the lily pad and into the water.

"Oh!" Aseneth said in surprise.

"The frogs here are a little shy. However, if you bring a few crumbs from dinner you can coax them out. The fish come up and beg too."

"Really? I'll remember to do that."

"Try it. It will be fun. It'll work better at the other end of the pool, there where the lily pads are. A fountain at this end flows in the evenings, so the frogs like the other end where it's a little quieter."

"Thank you so much for showing the pond to me."

"You'll want some things like that to do while you're here. The feasts sometimes last late into the night. They might not be as fun for you as they are for the others."

Asenath nodded. Grown-ups could be so dull sometimes. She looked at Joseph. He seemed to understand the kinds of things she would like. "Do you have a sister?" she shyly.

He smiled at her with his mouth, but his eyes looked sad. "Yes, but she lives far away from here."

"Do you miss her?"

"Sometimes. She and I used to do things like this. Although, when we did, I was the younger one. And it was her telling me the secrets."

"I wish I could meet her," Asenath said.

Joseph looked at her for a long time. "Yes, I imagine that you would enjoy her company. Both of you are surrounded by so many men, you would probably have a lot in common."

"Well, we'll just have to do it sometime."

"Let me show you where you and your father will be staying," he said, changing the subject. "Your servant will be along shortly with your things, and she'll help you get settled. Meanwhile, we have servants here, and I'll have one of them assist you." She followed him down a long pillared colonnade that led to a suite of rooms. "Your father will occupy that room there. And your servant will stay with you in this one. So at least you'll know where to find him."

"If he's ever in there," the girl sighed. "When he's on one of these trips he's always running around with the captain of the guard or Pharaoh or the general of the army or someone else."

Joseph laughed. "Yes, that's why he's here."

"Life, prosperity, and health," she said, then disappeared into her room.

* * *

The tall female slave bowed low. "I'm Aneksi and will serve you while you reside in the house of Potiphar."

Asenath spun around. She had taken off her wig and flung it on the table and was looking at a brightly colored wall painting. Coloring with embarrassment, she reached for the wig.

The slave smiled. "Don't be nervous. Many of the women take their wigs off when they're in their own apartments. They can be very heavy and hot after a while."

The girl sighed with relief. "Yes, and I'm not used to wearing one."

"I understand," the older woman said. "Where I came from, we never wore them. I had to get used to it when I arrived here. Once you adjust, it's not so bad."

Asenath relaxed a little. "You're not from here?"

"Well, I'm from here now. Most of the staff in the house of

Potiphar were purchased in the slave market, so we are from many places. I was of the Midianite tribe, but was sold into slavery after our village was raided and burned by another."

"Do you miss your family?"

"Yes," Aneksi replied, "but not as much as I did at first. I was just a little girl when I came here. That was a long time ago."

The girl nodded, then she thought of something else. "Is Joseph the son of Potiphar?"

The older woman started to laugh and than caught herself. "No, the wife of Potiphar has two sons, but they are very young."

"Oh. But he seems to be important here, and he's so nice."

The older woman smiled. "Yes, everyone has strong opinions about Joseph. They either love him or hate him."

"Hate him?" Asenath replied in surprise. "Why?"

"Well," the older woman lowered her voice confidentially, "when Joseph first came here, he was only a young man. You never saw such a homesick puppy. But he was purchased in the slave market just like the rest of us. He just always acted like he was—well, better than us."

"Really? He doesn't seem to be haughty."

"Not that, just, more intelligent—sophisticated perhaps. He's quite a thinker. Most of us gave up thinking when we were sold. Slaves do as they're told. Thinking is not a thing that is particularly safe to do."

The girl could understand that. No one liked an opinionated slave. "But Potiphar doesn't treat him like a slave. Why is that?"

"Joseph works very hard," Aneksi explained, "and he's very intelligent. He's also proved to be more honest and trustworthy than most, and worked up through the ranks of the slaves in a very short period of time. When Potiphar found out that he had different ideas about agriculture, and managing the farm and the crops, he let him experiment. The yield was so impressive that he put him in charge of all of the farmland. He's also over the household, an unusual thing for a man. He manages all of Potiphar's things now.

"Our master ceased regarding him as a slave long ago, and now treats him as a son. Until recently, when Potiphar married his current wife, he had no children. I suppose Joseph seemed to be the son he always wanted."

"So why do some people hate him?"

"I suppose it's jealousy," Aneksi said after a moment. "They feel that he's no better than any of the other slaves, yet he gets treated like family, and is honored and trusted and put over them when they were here first."

Asenath understood. She had seen plenty of that in her father's household too. The slaves all seemed to have a pecking order, and if someone didn't fit in, everyone would pick on them until they did.

"Anyway," the woman said, "such things are not for me to discuss. We all treat Joseph with respect, whether we like him or not."

"But you do respect him, don't you?"

"Of course! Now let's get you ready for dinner. Would you like a bath first?"

* * *

Asenath pushed the food around her plate. She had eaten all she wanted more than an hour ago, and yet the feast dragged on. Her father and the captain of the guard continued to chat about boring things such as irrigation and crop yields. "I've never been that much interested in farming," Potiphar said to her father. "It's something one must do to support the household and provide food. But digging in the dirt has never appealed to me."

The girl's father nodded. As a priest, he liked staying indoors and keeping his hands clean too. Neither man cared much for agriculture.

"So it was a great blessing when Joseph came up with all of these great ideas," he continued. "I guess for one who doesn't believe in worshiping Ra, the son god, or Hapy, the god of the annual flooding, one has to do other things to make sure the crops grow well. He expanded our irrigation system and planted the crops in different places during different seasons, and I don't know what else. But it has dramatically increased yield."

"Amazing."

"Yes, and he's done amazing things with the cattle. I've become a wealthy man, thanks to this slave of mine."

Potiphera, priest of On, nodded. "It's no small wonder then that you reward him with the status of a family member."

"I treat him well. He controls all of my land and estates. I feel that it's little repayment for the wealth he's brought me. And I've never had a slave that I felt I could fully trust—until Joseph."

Asenath's father nodded. Trustworthy slaves were few and far between. And trustworthy friends too, for that matter.

"I plan to give him his freedom, and a home and wife," Potiphar continued. "I just haven't gotten around to it yet."

The priest nodded. "He probably came from a well-bred background."

The palace official thought for a second. "I suppose so, though I never really inquired. But he was quite sophisticated even as a younger man. When he came, he already could read and write Canaanite script. It has been a great asset to him as a manager."

As the men continued to talk business, Asenath yawned. She wished that there were other girls to talk to. Potiphar's wife sat across the table from her, but she had ignored Aseneth since her arrival. She had been too busy flirting with the other men seated near her. When Aseneth looked around she saw that everyone else seemed to be enjoying the feast. Quietly she slipped from the table and left the room. *No one will notice anyway,* she thought. *And I've had enough of being a woman for this evening.* Racing down the hall, she went out into the courtyard. A full moon made it easy to see where she was going. She sat on the mud brick wall above the frog pond and watched the water ripple. After feeding the fish the crumbs she had saved from the table, she headed slowly toward the stables and slipped inside.

"You're a pretty fellow," she said as she stroked the nose of the horse next to her. "You look so big, but you were so gentle today." The horse snorted in apparent agreement. "I had a wonderful time when we were chariot-riding here. That was the most exciting thing I've done in my whole life." As she continued to stroke the animal, suddenly a low chuckle made her jump.

"I'm sure Charger appreciates all the attention," a voice said in the darkness, "but this isn't a safe place for you to come alone, especially at night."

"Come here," the man insisted. "It's just me." He stepped out from the darkness to where she could see him.

"Oh, Joseph, you scared me."

"Asenath, *you* scared me! When you disappeared from the banquet, I had the servants check everywhere in the house for you. No one could find you. Potiphar would be very upset if you got lost while you were here in his house."

"I'm not lost," she said indignantly, "I just came out here because it was boring in there."

Joseph laughed loudly. "I'm sure that's true, although I would never say that out loud in there. But you cannot come out here at night. It can be dangerous, and your safety is very important to everyone."

"Well," she said, "I'm safe now because you're here."

"Yes, I suppose you are."

"Then good. May I talk to Charger some more?"

"Sometimes animals can be the best company. I've spent a lot of time talking to them myself."

"Really? How long have you been here with Potiphar?"

"Several years. I was only 17 when I came."

Asenath thought a moment. "Tell me about your family."

"That can hardly interest you, my lady, daughter of the priest of On. My family were just shepherds."

"My father says that in other places shepherds are well respected and that some of them are even wealthy. It sounds strange to me, but he said it is so."

She could see Joseph nod in the moonlight. "Your father is right to say so. My father headed a shepherd clan. He had inherited great flocks and was wealthy."

"Then why are you a slave?" she blurted, then realizing what she had said, added, "You don't have to talk about it if you don't want to."

Joseph was quiet for several minutes. "I had a lot of older brothers," he said finally, "and there was a lot of jealousy in the family. It was a problem. I guess I did not understand how great a problem at the time."

"So what does that have to do with you being a slave?"

"I was my father's favorite. The one from his favorite wife, so I suppose the jealousy was there a little from the beginning, but it grew as I got older."

"So your brothers had something to do with you being here?"

"Yes. Most of them were much older. They were in charge of the flocks. Because our flocks were so large sometimes they had to take them many miles, to find adequate pasture."

Asenath nodded even though she knew nothing about shepherding at all.

"They had been gone for several weeks, and Father started worrying about them. He packed them some supplies and had me see if I could go find them to make sure they were well. It was hard to find them. They were supposed to be at Dothan, and I went there.

But they had gone, even though Father had not negotiated grazing rights anywhere else. A man there told me where to go look and I continued my journey. When I finally found them, they weren't happy to see me." A strange tone crept into his voice.

"What did they do?"

"They pushed me around a bit and threw me into a pit. I was afraid they were going to leave me there to die. Then a group of Midianite merchants came through. My brothers pulled me out and sold me to them for 20 pieces of silver—and here I am."

"You are lucky you were bought by Potiphar," Asenath announced. "He is one of the wealthiest men in Egypt."

"I don't consider it luck," he said softly.

* * *

It had been many months since the disappearance of Joseph. Asenath no longer looked forward to her trips to Avaris with her father, but she continued to accompany him although her father made arrangements for her to stay in Pharaoh's household when they were in town. She made friends with the other women at court and realized that she was being groomed for a political marriage.

Asenath sighed as the slave girl put her wig into place and began to paint her eyelids. "Do you ever wish you were a princess?" she asked the slave.

"Not when I'm working, my lady," the slave replied respectfully. "I try very hard just to keep my mind on my work and not wish anything, but in the night sometimes I have dreams that I am pretty and important and people are serving me instead of me serving them."

"Sometimes I have dreams of being an unimportant child of a peasant. Then I would have so much more freedom. I could do what I wanted to, go where I wanted to, fall in love with whom I wanted to."

The slave girl was quiet. "I suppose," she said, "though I haven't found life to be that way."

"No, I don't suppose that you have. I guess I never wished I was a slave—just . . . " She sighed again and left her thoughts unspoken.

The slave girl smiled. "My brother is a slave too," she said.

"Really?" the girl said, only half interested.

"Yes, he works over at the prison."

Asenath's ears perked up. "He does? What does he do there?"

"He's in charge of bringing food and supplies to the governor of the jail and delivering messages for him."

"What does he tell you about life at the jail?"

"Well," the slave girl continued, smiling slightly, "he says that a slave of Potiphar, who was sent there, is quite gifted in administration."

"Really?"

"Apparently he was while he was working for Potiphar, too, for he had been put in charge of the entire household."

"Yes," Asenath said, "we used to go there for feasts and I met him several times—if he's the same one."

The slave girl nodded. "Well, he has done the same thing in the jail. He has continued to be promoted until he runs the place. From what my brother tells me, he seems to be a good person. Not only is the governor of the jail pleased with him, but the prisoners seem happier too. Apparently others who have worked under the governor have played favorites and embezzled food that was to go to the prisoners and mistreated those they didn't care for. Joseph seems to be very fair-minded and treats the prisoners much better than they ever have been. Which is a good thing, because my brother says that with most of them being political prisoners, they will not be there long. If they have been treated well, they may not harbor such ill feelings toward Pharaoh or the governor of the prison when released."

Asenath nodded. So Joseph was still alive and doing well. He was still the same person that she had come to know—consistent, fair, and always an astute leader. "He sounds like a good man." She kept her eyes on the mirror she held before her, watching the slave apply her makeup, but inside she was bursting with joy. What if Joseph's God really did exist? What if he really was higher than her own gods? Joseph always believed his God knew where he was and had him there for a purpose. Could he have a purpose even in Pharaoh's jail? The girl didn't know, but hope sprung anew in her heart.

Later, when she was alone, she closed her eyes and whispered, "God of Joseph, if You are there—and Joseph believes that You are and I'm beginning to believe that You are—please protect him and care for him, and bring him back to me somehow. I don't know how this could be, but Joseph says you can do anything, and I believe him." She stared at the night sky. Would Joseph's God hear her? While she didn't know, she did lay down on her sleeping mat with a new peace in her heart.

* * *

"Asenath," her father said, "the next two days are going to be dangerous. I want you to stay in your quarters here in the palace. Do not go out. Do not go visit anyone. Stay right here."

"Why, what's happening?"

"A conspiracy is brewing. Potiphar, the captain of the guard, and I have known about it for a short time. There will be arrests made and there may be some bloodshed and violence."

"Even here in the palace?" she asked incredulously.

"Even here in the palace," he replied sadly. "Trust no one and speak of this to no one. Just keep to yourself, stay in your chambers, and do not come out until I send for you."

"I will—I will not mention this to anyone." Being the daughter of an important official, she was used to keeping secrets. *I wonder what is happening?* she thought after returning to her chamber. *What kind of conspiracy? Against whom? Against her father? Against Pharaoh? Against Egypt?*

The day continued quietly until that evening. Then she suddenly heard muffled shouts and the sounds of running feet down the hall. Asenath stayed in her chamber as instructed and Senetenpu dropped the large beam across the door into its slots so no one could enter. They sat there quietly, straining to hear what was happening in the palace. More shouts came from many directions.

Apparently, Potiphar had planned the ambush well, catching the conspirators off guard. The shouting and scuffling quickly ended, and soon Asenath heard a tap at the door.

When her father called her name, she and her servant pushed the beam up and flung the door open. "Father, I'm so glad you're safe. I heard commotion in the hall and was worried about you."

He hugged her. "I was worried about you, too. That's why I wanted you to stay in your room. It is safe to come out now."

"What happened?"

"A conspiracy against Pharaoh sought to assassinate him and take over the government. However, we surprised them."

"Where are they? What did you do with them?"

"Well, the ringleader is dead, and so are many of those who tried to defend him. Others have been put in the prison until we can determine whether they were involved or not. Many arrests have been made, and it will probably take us weeks to work through everything and separate the innocent from the guilty. But the captain of the guard does his job well, and his information sources are apparently reliable and accurate."

"What a relief for us," Asenath said, smiling at her father.

"I will be very busy for the next few weeks with the trials in Pharaoh's court, so we'll be here a while. I wanted you and Senetenpu to know it was safe to come out now and that you may do whatever it is you women do during the daytime."

Asenath laughed. "You know it's nothing interesting, Father—that's why I like following you around."

He nodded. "I understand—it doesn't sound interesting to me, either, but if you're going to make a good marriage, you need to know a few womanly things, and I'm afraid those are things I can't teach you." Bidding her good night, he headed down the hall.

Asenath leaned against the wall, staring up at the night sky through the little window just below the ceiling. "God of Joseph," she whispered, "thank You for protecting us and thank You for protecting my father. After all, it couldn't have been Ra. He's gone to bed!" She giggled at her little joke, then she and Senetenpu went to bed too.

The next morning Asenath watched for Merit, the young slave girl whose brother worked in the prison. By afternoon she had found her and asked if she could borrow her to help her with her preparations for the evening's social activities. As the young slave girl painted the dark kohl along her eyelids, Asenath asked nonchalantly, "Is your brother a lot busier now with the prison so full?"

"Oh, yes," Merit laughed. "He says he's been running errands so fast he meets himself coming and going."

"I'm sure he's very busy. However, it must be quite interesting."

"Do you know that the chief butler is in there, and so is the baker? It seems all kinds of people were in on the conspiracy."

"They haven't decided yet, have they, who were conspirators and who might have been innocent?"

"Not yet, but everyone suspected has been put in jail. They're probably all guilty."

"Really? It would be pretty scary to imagine that the person in charge of all the royal food and drink was involved. What if they poisoned everyone at court?" Asenath shuddered—it was not something she wanted to think about.

She wondered if Joseph were talking to those men now and whether he could tell who was innocent and guilty. Then she remembered the dreams he had told her he had had when he was still at home and how he believed the one God might speak to him through dreams. They were odd dreams for a young son to have— even odder for a slave. Who knew what the one God planned for Joseph? Maybe the one God would let Joseph know who was innocent and who was guilty. Asenath did not care what they did with the guilty conspirators, but the idea of someone innocent being punished greatly disturbed her.

"God of Joseph," she whispered at her window, "I hope You don't mind me talking to You all the time. I just miss Joseph so much, and it's comforting to me to know that he and I both talk to You. Joseph says that You know what's inside of everyone's heart. You know who's innocent and guilty. Please do something to protect the innocent—and that includes Joseph. I know You have a plan for him. Please help the others. I will always worship You if You can help me with this. Even if I never see Joseph again."

* * *

"Asenath," her father said, "tomorrow will be your birthday. I'm sorry I've been so involved in the courts of Pharaoh here for so long, but with the conspiracy hearings it will be longer before we will be able to go back to On where we can celebrate as we used to. In the meantime, is there anything I can buy you that will amuse you?"

His daughter paused for a moment. "Do you think you could buy the young slave Merit from Pharaoh?" she asked. "I like her— she amuses me."

"Certainly. I'll ask him today. And thanks for being so understanding. We will do something fun when we go home to celebrate the times we're missing now. Meanwhile, I'm glad you found someone to amuse you here at court."

Asenath smiled to herself. Merit would be her link to the prison. If she were her slave, she would get to hear news from there all the time. It made her feel a little closer to Joseph. At least, she would know what he was doing and if all was well with him.

Father was as good as his word and approached Pharaoh about the young slave, but when the ruler realized it was Asenath's birthday, he refused to sell Merit to his priest. He gave her as a gift instead.

Clapping her hands in delight, Asenath cried, "Oh, thank you, thank you, Your Majesty!" Merit seemed pleased too, although she kept her gaze centered on the floor.

Later that night as Senetenpu was putting her to bed, Asenath asked her, "Do you think Merit was happy to be given to me? It must not feel good to be given to someone if you had no choice in the matter."

"Well, she has no choice in the matter," Senetenpu, always a very practical woman, pointed out.

"Do you think she'll be happy with us?"

The woman stared at her for a long moment. "You know nothing of the lives of slaves. Happiness isn't really a word that most slaves know the meaning of. Merit has not been particularly well treated, being one of the younger and less important slaves here at court. She's homesick for her family. Her life will be much better with you, and maybe someday she might even be happy, but that really isn't a word in the vocabulary of a slave, you know."

Asenath stared at the wall hours after Senetenpu left. It was true she didn't know what being a slave was like. She had always been wealthy, well treated, and well fed. Many times she had noticed lash marks on the backs of slaves, and she had seen some women slap their slaves for even small infractions. But she had just never thought about the issue before. What would it be like to be a slave? Although she tried, she just couldn't imagine—but Joseph knew.

As always her mind turned to him and she wondered what he was doing and hoped he was sleeping by now—this late at night.

The next morning young Merit was already there with warm

water for her bath and makeup for her face when Asenath woke up. She chattered away happily as she assisted her new mistress with her morning routine.

"I'm kind of glad my father was so busy with the hearings even if I didn't get to go home for my birthday," Asenath told her, "otherwise they never would have given you to me."

Merit looked self-conscious. "It is an honor to serve you, Lady Asenath. Does this mean I will go with you when you return to On?"

"Of course." Then Asenath saw a look of pain flash across the girl's face. "Why, what's the matter? On is a wonderful place. You'll love it. It's my home, it's where I grew up, and it's much more comfortable there than here." Then she stopped. It was her home but it wasn't Merit's. "Oh, your brother is here."

Merit nodded, her eyes welling with tears.

"Well, as your mistress, I will make sure you have duties that will take you by the prison."

The slave girl's eyes lit up. "You would do that?"

"Of course. And I will go with you. I'll get my father to arrange a bodyguard for us."

"Oh, thank you, my lady." A tear spilled down her cheek, and she brushed it away quickly. "You are very generous to me."

"Perhaps, if I'm needing another present—just perhaps, Father might buy your brother for me."

"Really?"

"Yes, but for now, let's figure out a way for you to see him at least once in a while. Though we go back to On, we are frequent visitors in Avaris and of the court."

"Yes, you are my lady. Will I be allowed to accompany you when you come to court?"

"Of course. Who else would do my makeup?"

It was only days before Asenath had arranged a trip to the market located near the prison entrance. With an approved bodyguard,

Merit and her brother chatted happily as Asenath browsed in the market, thumping melons, examining cucumbers, and looking at all the imported fabrics and jewelry, spices, and art objects brought in by the traders on the Nile trading vessels.

However, she kept her eyes averted from the far wall, the site of the slave market. The slave market wasn't as exciting as it used to be since she had become a friend with Merit and Joseph. She wondered how many other slaves being sold there had families and friends that they missed—perhaps all of them. The thought made her shudder.

After returning to their quarters in the palace, Merit was bursting with news. "Lady Asenath, Ani, my brother, told me all kinds of things from the prison. It's really exciting there with all the trials going on and the investigations. The butler and the baker are in there, plus a bunch of people who aren't as important and whom I've never heard of."

"What has been happening?"

"Well, the butler and the baker both had dreams that they thought were very significant, but they couldn't figure out their meanings, so they told them to Joseph, the supervisor of the jail."

"Ah," Asenath said, smiling to herself. "Yes, I've heard of him." They both grinned at each other, though neither one understood totally why the other one was smiling. "The butler told Joseph that he had dreamed that he was squeezing grapes into Pharaoh's cup again and Pharaoh drank from the cup. Joseph told him that the branches on the vine he dreamed about meant that in three days something would happen. Pharaoh would call him back into court, and he would be found innocent and get to return to his job.

"This made the baker really excited, so he told Joseph that he also had a dream. In it he had three baskets on top of his head filled with pastries that Pharaoh loved. Some birds flew down and snatched some food out of his top basket.

"He was hoping for an exciting interpretation like the butler had, but Joseph told him it meant that in three days Pharaoh would bring him back to court, find him guilty, and have him beheaded."

"Beheaded!" Asenath exclaimed.

"So everyone in the prison is excited and can't wait to find out whether Joseph's interpretations come true or not."

Asenath smiled. "So he's not just a dreamer but an interpreter of dreams."

"What? He dreams them too?" Merit asked. "Is that what you meant?"

"Oh, never mind," Asenath said, realizing that she had already said too much.

* * *

It was a long three days. On the morning of the third day, Asenath asked, "Father, may Merit and I come to the hall of justice with you?"

"Of course, since it's a public hearing, but are you sure you wouldn't find it too upsetting?"

"I'm just curious to see what happens." She explained to her father the dreams about the butler and the baker.

"Interesting," the priest murmured. "The butler is scheduled for his hearing today, but we don't plan to do the baker's case until tomorrow."

"May I come?"

"Yes. If you get bored, though, then just let me know and I'll have some servants bring you back here."

Merit and Asenath could hardly sit still in their excitement. Asenath had never been to a legal session before. Until then she had never cared about such things, but now she was interested. She stood with other members of Pharaoh's household on one side near the front, where she could see what took place.

Guards brought the butler in with his arms bound. Scribes presented evidence both on his behalf and against him. Both her father and Potiphar, chief of the king's guard, stood by Pharaoh's throne listening and occasionally murmuring to each other or to him. When the scribes finished, Pharaoh raised his hand and spoke.

"I find you not guilty of the crimes of conspiracy. You will be restored to your previous position. Your land and your home will be restored to you. I find you to be a loyal servant."

"Oh, thank you, my lord," the butler said, falling on his face before the king. Then he stood to his feet and the guards untied his arms. Bowing once more, he then turned and walked from the courtroom.

"Merit," Asenath whispered, "it's just as Joseph said it would be."

The slave girl nodded. "But this is the third day—what about the baker?"

Potiphar, chief of the king's guard, then spoke to Pharaoh. "We had two other cases scheduled for this afternoon, but apparently the two got in a fight during the night. One has died, and the other is severely injured."

Pharaoh nodded.

"Do you wish to stop for today," Potiphar continued, "or do you wish to hear one of tomorrow's cases? The next one would be that of your baker."

"Bring him in. We will take the midday rest; then I will hear his case."

Asenath turned and met Merit's eyes. It was going to happen today—the third day—just as Joseph said. The girl closed her eyes. She was afraid to whisper out loud, but Joseph had said that the one God could hear prayers even inside a person's heart. *God of Joseph, I thank You for making a way for this innocent man to be spared. You are good even to my people,* she thought, hoping Joseph's God listened to her words.

* * *

It had been two years since the conspiracy trials. Asenath continued to travel with her father, though her older servant, Senetenpu, sometimes stayed in their home in On. She had been a faithful servant for years, and now her health was failing. Even though Asenath reduced the woman's duties, the young woman's father still made sure the servant was well taken care of. On each visit to Avaris, Asenath arranged a trip to the market where they just happened to meet Ani, Merit's brother, to hear more news from the prison.

It had been such a visit. Asenath was lying on her bed in her palace apartments, trying to go to sleep. Usually the nights were cool along the Nile, but tonight was hot, with no breeze anywhere. She rose and went to the little window. "God of Joseph," she whispered, thinking how it no longer seemed strange to talk to the foreign deity, she had come to do it so frequently. "I wish I knew what Your plans were. While I am sure that You have one for him, he's been in the prison for several years now. Joseph says You have perfect timing for everything and that he trusts You. I know You are taking good care of him in the prison, and even though Pharaoh will probably marry me off to some court official's son (or whomever he's making a political alliance with at the time), I believe You'll take good care of Joseph and lead him out of the prison to wherever Your heart plans for him to be."

A commotion somewhere else in the palace interrupted her prayer. Soon she heard loud voices, and raising herself up so she could see out the window, watched torches cross a courtyard. She could see that the royal quarters were bright with light.

"I guess Pharaoh can't sleep tonight either," she murmured. Soon the sounds of running footsteps approached, and someone knocked on her door. She pulled a shawl around her shoulders and opened her door, peeking into the shadows beyond. Her father's bodyguard was already nodding curtly to the slave on the other side. Asenath immediately followed Merit to her father's room, where she saw that he had hastily dressed.

"What is it, Father?"

"Go back to bed, daughter. Pharaoh is having dreams from the gods, and I must help him understand their meaning. All is well. It's not another conspiracy or assassination attempt. Everything's all right."

Although Asenath returned to her room, now she was even more wide awake. She stared up through the little window at the top of the wall. What kind of message would Pharaoh be receiving that he could not understand himself? After all, he was Horus incarnate on earth—a god—and able to understand the words of the other gods.

Suddenly an idea struck her. If Father and the other priests could not give the king an interpretation, perhaps Joseph could. *No,* she thought, *what a silly idea. They won't listen to someone in prison. Yet, perhaps—* She paced back and forth. It was several hours before she finally fell into a restless sleep.

Asenath woke up tired and with a headache. When she joined her father for breakfast he looked even worse.

"It turned out to be a short night, didn't it, Father?"

"Yes, a terrible night."

"Did you help Pharaoh get back to sleep?"

"No," he said curtly.

"You weren't able to tell him the meaning of his dream?"

"No."

"Was anyone else able to?"

He stared at her. "What makes you so full of questions this morning?"

Asenath looked at her melon chunks on her plate and pushed them around with her finger. She wasn't hungry. "My slave has a brother who works in the prison," she began.

"Yes," he snapped.

"Well, the butler and the baker had dreams in prison and the supervisor of the prison there was able to interpret them for them."

"Really?" he said, totally uninterested as he glanced at an open papyrus scroll next to him. "So you're wanting me to buy him as a slave for you too?"

Asenath laughed. "Of course not." She kept only a female slave, though they had male slaves back at their home in On. "No, but I was thinking that since both of his interpretations came true, Pharaoh might ask him about his dream."

"Enough of this impertinence!" her father roared, slamming his fist down on the scroll. "If I, the high priest of Ra, and all the other priests of all the other gods of Egypt were unable to interpret Pharaoh's dream, why would you even suggest some slave from the prisons?"

"He's in charge of the whole prison."

Then he seemed to calm himself. "I'm sorry, Asenath," he said less loudly. "I didn't mean to shout at you, but sometimes the things you say are just ridiculous." He glanced at his food. "I'm not hungry." He strode from the room.

Asenath put her head in her hands. "I tried," she whispered.

* * *

In the royal apartments Pharaoh's breakfast was as unappealing to him as Asenath's had been to her. Though I stayed with Asenath, for she was my charge, I was able to hear much more acutely than humans were.

"This wine tastes sour!" Pharaoh shouted, flinging his cup on the floor and splattering the butler with the juice.

"Your Majesty, I will bring you some other wine immediately."

"Forget it," the king growled. "I don't want anything. I have things to do today. Leave me."

The butler, trembling, glanced back and forth rapidly from the Pharaoh to the door. Should he speak or should he run? He spoke. "I had a dream in prison," he said, "before you heard my case and graciously set me free and restored me to my office."

"Did you now?" Pharaoh said curtly but with a shred of interest. "What did you dream?"

"The dream was not as important, my Lord, as the interpretation. There is an interpreter of dreams in the prison who told me not only a meaning of my dream but also that of the baker."

"He interpreted dreams for a traitor who planned to kill me. Who is this villain?"

The butler bowed low. "No, my lord, he is no villain. He told me that in three days I would be acquitted and set free and restored. Then he foretold the baker's death, and even the method of execution. And all of these things happened just as he said."

He had Pharaoh's total interest now. By this time Potiphar, the chief of the king's guards, and Potiphera, the high priest of On, had both entered the royal apartments.

"Listen to this," Pharaoh said, commanding the butler to repeat his story. Both men's eyes widened as they listened. And both turned pale.

"You know of this man?" the priest of On whispered to the chief of the king's guards, who also had charge of the prison.

Potiphar nodded. "Yes, he was my slave. He was the manager of my estates. I had him imprisoned. It was a very bad situation, though I am certain he was innocent. This is very awkward."

The high priest of On nodded. "That it is, especially as I recall from the things I've been told, this man does not worship any Egyptian gods."

The chief of the king's guard shook his head. "No, he worships some desert God."

"So if none of us could interpret the dream and he does, this could cause the priesthood some problems too."

Both men turned to their ruler to give him their opinions, but it was too late.

"Have him brought to me at once," Pharaoh said. "No, have him bathed and shaved. Let him interpret the dream not as a barbarian but with dignity—if he can. If he can interpret it at all. We will wait."

The two officials' eyes met and their jaws clenched. They dreaded the difficult day ahead of them.

"Asenath," her father called as he entered their quarters in the palace.

"I'm here. What's the matter?"

"Repeat to me again what you told me at breakfast about the young man in the prison. Tell me everything you know about him."

Asenath paled, but she and her father sat down. She related everything she could remember—the story of his family, of the massacre at Shechem, and of his brothers selling Joseph into slavery.

Her father nodded. "All this fits with the other information I have received about this man. So he interprets dreams. Accurately?"

"Yes, but he says that the one God gives him the interpretation."

"Whatever. And he had dreams of everyone bowing to him someday?"

Asenath nodded.

"I believe this dream is about to come true, and if it does there may be serious problems for us."

"Why? Joseph would never hurt us."

"Wouldn't he? He's a slave, brought here against his will."

"But he was very loyal to Potiphar."

"Was he?" the priest asked. "Wasn't he jailed for attacking Potiphar's wife?"

"But he didn't do it," she protested.

The priest of On paused for a moment. "You're probably right. I'm afraid this will be an interesting day. Come with me back to the court."

Asenath stood with Merit and other royalty in Pharaoh's court. The king, complete with full ceremonial headdress sat on his golden throne. Potiphera, the high priest of On, and Potiphar, captain of the guard, stood next to him. Everyone waited in silence. Then the throne room doors opened and Joseph walked in, flanked by the guards. Pharaoh was too impatient to deal with the usual formal greetings.

"My butler tells me you interpret dreams correctly."

"No, my lord," Joseph replied. "I don't—but the one God whom I serve is able to interpret dreams and everything that happens in the human heart, and He can give you the meaning of this dream."

Pharaoh studied the foreign slave for a few moments as if he was unsure whether to trust Joseph or not. Then he made up his mind. "What I dreamed was this: Seven cows grazed in my pasture. They were big strong healthy cows and looked fine. Then seven starving and ugly cows emerged from the river. They walked up to my seven good cows and ate them. Cows do not eat other cows. It just makes no sense to me.

"Then I fell asleep and dreamed a second time. I had a field of grain and in it were seven ears of grain that looked ready to harvest. Healthy, full ears of grain. Then seven ears of grain came out of the river. Diseased and shriveled, they looked as if they hadn't had enough rain and that perhaps insects and other things had attacked them. Although they ate the seven good ears of grain, they still looked as shriveled as ever."

Joseph nodded.

"Well," Pharaoh said after a pause, "what does it mean?" Every eye focused on him and Joseph. It seemed that everyone in the court was holding his or her breath. The two Potiphars watched in anxious silence. Asenath's heart felt as if it was pounding in her throat. Merit, pale, bit her bottom lip.

"The one God says this dream has been sent you as a warning," Joseph said at last. "Right now you have prosperity in Egypt. Your cattle are healthy, your crops are good, and no one is hungry. This will continue for seven years. After seven years there will be a terrible famine that will also last seven years. The one God is sending you this warning because He cares for you and the people of Egypt."

Pharaoh thought a moment. "What does He want me to do?"

Joseph paused, then said, "It would be wise to appoint someone to prepare for this time. You could impose a tax—say 20 percent of the crops—and have them brought to central storehouses. This person should oversee construction of appropriate storage bins. Perhaps building them far enough from the Nile so that its annual flooding will not affect them, but close enough that the grain can be shipped by boat to different parts of Egypt during the famine. If you construct storage areas close to the quarries and line them with plaster, they should stay dry, and once sealed, rodents and robbers will not be able to get to them as easily. The person overseeing them could then accept the grain taxes from the people for the seven years. The people also should be told to store grain on their own farms. After the seven years of plenty, Egypt will have a huge amount of grain in storage belonging to you, O King. Then when your people are hungry, you can sell them grain and they will not starve. Egypt will be strong. The famine will also be in the other nations surrounding you, and they will come to you for food."

The king seemed lost in thought. "Not only would Pharaoh be able to take care of his people," he said finally, "but it would also strengthen Egypt's position among surrounding countries."

"One is always blessed this way when one follows the plans of the one God," Joseph said. The captain of the guard and the priest of On's eyes widened, but they said nothing.

Again Pharaoh thought for a moment, then started to laugh. "We have many gods in Egypt, but today it seems that your God cares more about my kingdom than any of the rest of them."

The priest of On bit his lip.

"You may tell your God that I appreciate His warning. I shall do as He suggested. Now I need to appoint a man to oversee this project."

Joseph bowed and turned to leave.

"Pharaoh commands that you stay." Looking less confident, Joseph again faced the king. Both Potiphar and Potiphera had broken into a cold sweat, and now Joseph looked as uncomfortable as they did. The king stood and strode across the room toward Joseph.

"I appoint you," he suddenly announced. "You obviously have the ear of the one God. I understand from the stories my servants tell that you are gifted in administrative skills." He turned to his chief of security. "And that you made Potiphar a rich man."

Joseph seemed to be studying his left big toe carefully. Potiphar, chief of the king's guard, wiped his forehead nervously.

"Well?"

"Yes, Your Majesty," Joseph answered.

"Is this not true?" The king turned to Potiphar.

"Yes, my lord."

The king pulled off his signet ring with the large scarab on it and handed it to Joseph. "Put this on. Joseph, you are second in command in my entire kingdom, answerable only to me. You will do all these things as your God suggested and will manage Egypt for me. I have many responsibilities for my people. This will give me an opportunity to deal with them while you prepare the country for the coming famine."

Pharaoh reached behind his neck and undid the clasp of the heavy jewel-studded gold collar he wore. "This is for you too," he said, handing it to a guard who fastened it on Joseph. The former slave stood in stunned silence. "For the time being you will live here in the palace until we can arrange for a suitable home for you. You'll receive servants and everything you need," he said.

Turning to the chief of his household servants, he ordered, "Please see that appropriate changes of clothing and furnishings are supplied to this man and take care of whatever he requires.

"Now you may leave," Pharaoh said. Joseph bowed low, not knowing what to say.

As Joseph again started to leave, Pharaoh declared, "One more thing." Joseph paused and looked at him expectantly. Asenath's heart skipped a beat. Would Pharaoh change his mind? She could hardly breathe.

"You need a noble wife. I give you Lady Asenath, daughter of the high priest of On." Joseph glanced across where the young woman stood in shocked silence. Then he broke into a huge smile. Asenath nodded faintly toward him and bowed to Pharaoh.

"Does that meet with your approval?" he asked.

Joseph nodded.

"What is your name?" Pharaoh demanded. "I almost forgot to ask!"

"I am Joseph."

"From now on you'll be known as Zaphnath-paaneah." A murmur rippled through the court. Joseph was now to be known as "the god speaks that he [Joseph] may live." The pharaoh of Egypt was giving a token of respect to the one God with his second in command's new name.

"Well," Pharaoh said, "go! You have work to do."

"Yes, my lord," Joseph replied with a smile as he turned and left the court.

"Well," Pharaoh continued, turning to the two Potiphars, "you also have work to do. We have a royal wedding to plan. Go, go." The two perspiring men hastened from the room.

Asenath returned to her quarters in a state of shock. There she found her father and Potiphar, chief of the king's guards, in deep discussion. When she entered the apartment they both stood and bowed.

"What?" she started to ask, then realized that as Joseph's wife, she outranked both men. "Oh, sit down, Father," she said. "We've got to talk." Both men seated themselves and looked at her nervously. "You have nothing to fear from my"—she blushed at the word—"husband."

"What makes you think so?" her father asked.

"Joseph is a good man. He is fair, and the one God is fair too."

The two men looked unconvinced. "Will you come with us to Joseph's chambers? I mean, Zaphnath-phaaneah's?" Potiphar, chief of security, asked. "We need to find out what he is going to do to us, and I would rather find out now."

"Yes," her father added. "At least we can do this with dignity."

Asenath suddenly realized that they were looking to her for protection. "Let's go," she said, leading the way. "The one God has taken care of everything else. He'll be merciful to us, too," she said softly.

I smiled to myself and followed. The Almighty One was saving not only the children of Abraham, but the people of Egypt as well. His desire was to save and protect all His human children. But the children of Abraham would go through some amazing experiences yet.

MAHLEENDAH

xciting things were afoot in Egypt. Pharaoh's daughter had rescued a Hebrew baby from the death decree her father had ordered against all the baby boys, and then she had raised him in the palace as her own son. All of us watchers were pretty certain that he was the promised one who would lead the Israelites out of Egypt and away from their slavery. So it was with mixed feelings that I received my present assignment.

My charge is out in the Sinai Desert, the daughter of Jethro, a shepherd-priest of Midian who worships the one God. He is also a descendant of Abraham's son by his second wife, Keturah. As a worshiper of the Almighty, Jethro received the same blessings and protection and so it came to be that heaven assigned me to his daughter Mahleendah.

Although blessed with seven beautiful daughters, Jethro had no sons. Life as a desert sheepherder was difficult without sons, and so his daughters had to fill that role until such a time as they were old enough to marry so that their father would have sons-in-law. Of course, this posed problems of its own since by custom they would join the families of their husbands. Jethro tried not to think about that, and meanwhile I concentrated on recording the choices of one of the younger daughters.

Zipporah, Mahleendah's older sister, was in charge of the flocks. Four of the other sisters went along to help her each day. Mahleendah and one younger sister stayed home and took care of the cooking and other home duties, but in the afternoons when Zipporah and the other girls brought the sheep back, they would join them at the well to help draw water for them. Watering the sheep was a backbreaking job, and it always amazed Mahleendah how much the wooly animals could drink.

As if drawing water from the deep well was not trial enough, they also had to deal with Eliphaz and his friends. Eliphaz cared for a flock of sheep that grazed close by. Every day when the girls would bring their sheep to the well before they took them home to their enclosure for the night, Eliphaz would bully the girls. Sometimes he would shove them out of the way while he watered his flock first, making them wait even though they were there first. Other times he would force them to draw water for his sheep as well.

Mahleendah cringed inside every time she saw him coming. Yet she could do little about it. Her father said that they couldn't afford to have hostile relations with the Amelakite family of whom Eliphaz was a part. For now they would just have to share the water and do their best to avoid the man.

Today when Mahleendah and her younger sister approached the well they noticed someone already there. They paused and stared at the man sleeping in the scant shade of a small bush.

"He looks like an Egyptian," Mahleendah whispered.

Her little sister nodded. "But he's all alone. Nobody travels through the desert all alone."

Mahleendah thought about that fact. It was far too dangerous because of bandits and other threats. Anyone making a journey usually joined a group of merchants for safety in numbers. The girls crept around to the other side of the well to get a better look at the stranger.

"Well, whoever he is, he's very handsome," Mahleendah said quietly. Just then they heard the sound of sheep. Moments later Zipporah, with her flock of sisters and sheep, rounded the bend in the wadi and approached the well. Still the Egyptian appeared to sleep.

Ignoring him completely, Zipporah headed for the well. "Look at this, girls," she said, "we've made it to the well before Eliphaz. Perhaps if we work fast, we can get our sheep watered before he gets here."

The girls laughed and swarmed around the well, tugging the ropes that held the heavy goatskin bucket of water as they raised it and dumped it into the trough for their animals to drink. "Maybe you should just come early a few minutes everyday," Mahleendah suggested. "It doesn't give the sheep as long to graze, but it sure would be worth it."

"Why have you started without me?" a male voice suddenly demanded.

Zipporah's shoulders sagged as she looked up. "Eliphaz, what a surprise."

"On the contrary," he replied, "it seems that it is you that has prepared a lovely surprise for me—already filling the trough for my animals to drink."

"This surprise was not for you," she countered. "The water is for our animals."

"Oh, I don't think so," he said, continuing his feigned politeness. He nodded to the boys with him. With their staffs they pushed Zipporah's sheep away and guided their own to the troughs.

"Eliphaz, that's not fair!" Zipporah protested. "You know how much work it is to pull up all that water. We did that for our sheep."

He smirked. "I do know how much work it is. That's why I'm so grateful. Now if you'll step out of the way."

"No!" she shouted.

He shoved Zipporah to the side.

The Egyptian, who had roused from his sleep, now strode to the well. Lifting Zipporah back to her feet, he smiled at the girls and then turned to Eliphaz. "I couldn't help overhearing," he said.

I smiled to myself, knowing who had been sleeping beneath the shrub, for I recognized his guardian. Not only did his charge best the other shepherds in a three to one fight, but made them draw water for the girls' flocks. I chuckled. His temper may be too short to lead the children of Jacob out of their slavery at this point in time, but it certainly came in handy for defending my charge, who now stood with her mouth hanging open. For that matter so did all her sisters.

When their flocks had finished drinking, they thanked him and hurried away, leaving their benefactor standing by the well with the three shepherds who now had to draw water for their own flocks.

* * *

"You left him where? At the well, with those Amlekites, alone?" Jethro, their father, shouted. "What were you thinking? Where's your sense of hospitality? Your mother would be ashamed. Go back and get him at once."

The girls scrambled from the tent. "Mahleendah, you and Serina make sure we have food prepared. The rest of us will go back and get him."

"We want to go too," Mahleendah complained, but Zipporah was already hurrying down the path. The girl sighed, and, grabbing young Serina by the hand, headed over toward the cooking fire.

"We should probably bake more bread, too," she said to her sister, eyeing the small stack of flat bread she and her sister had made that afternoon. "We don't want to run out. I would hate for that Egyptian man to consider us poor hosts."

Serina smiled. "I'll help you. Let's do it right away. Maybe we can get some of those dried figs out of the cave too. This is a special occasion."

From their vantage point they could see Zipporah talking to the Egyptian and then watched as the two of them headed back toward father's tent. "I wonder who he is," Mahleendah whispered. "Did you see his hands? They don't look like he's done a day's work in his life."

"But he's so strong," her sister protested. "Did you see those muscles?"

"Of course," the older girl said haughtily. "He had to have muscles to defeat all three shepherds at once." Both girls giggled. "Wasn't that great—and he made them draw all the water for us."

"It was only fair after all the times they've made us water their flocks!"

The girls soon finished their meal preparation and headed to their father's tent. They crouched behind it where they could hear what was being said.

"So how did you come to be crossing the desert alone?" they heard their father ask.

"It's a long story," the Egyptian replied, not offering to tell it.

"Had some trouble in Egypt?" It was half a question, half an answer from Jethro. Mahleendah frowned, wishing she could see their faces as they talked.

"You are welcome to stay with us for as long as you wish," their father offered.

"I thank you for your hospitality," the Egyptian answered.

"You know," Jethro's voice came again, "I was blessed with beautiful daughters but I have no sons. It would be good to have another man in the family. If you choose to stay and help the girls—as you did today—I would be more than grateful."

Mahleendah yelped as she suddenly felt herself lifted off her feet by a hand on the back of her robe. "What do you think you're doing?" Zipporah scolded. "You know that eavesdropping is rude! Give Father his privacy to talk to the Egyptian. Bring the food, for he will be staying for dinner."

The two younger girls scampered back to the cooking fire and then looked over their shoulder to see Zipporah listening from the vantage point they had had just moments before.

"Do you think he'll stay?" Serina asked.

"I don't know. I hope so."

I looked at the Egyptian's guardian. He shrugged. "Where else would he go?" he asked me. I didn't know either but was glad he was staying in the tents of Jethro since I knew the Almighty had important plans for this one, and I was glad he was near enough that I could be in on the action.

* * *

It had been several months since the handsome Egyptian had joined their family clan. He was quiet and didn't talk about himself much, but Mahleendah had learned his name was Moses, a good Egyptian name. It was a little confusing, though, to watch him, when Father offered the evening sacrifices to the one God, Moses seemed to be worshiping too, and he was constantly asking questions. Father would sit for hours at the campfire in the evenings telling him the stories Mahleendah and her sisters had grown up on—stories of Adam and Eve, of Noah and his family, and of Abraham, their ancestor.

He also inquired about the other side of the family—about the sons of Isaac and of Jacob. Jethro told him all of the stories he knew and answered every question as honestly as possible. One evening as Mahleendah was bringing the food to the men at the campfire, she heard Jethro say, "So, Moses, how long are you going to be content just to be a stranger among us? Why don't you marry my oldest daughter and be the heir of my flocks and of the clan?"

Mahleendah dropped a bread basket with a clatter, but neither Moses nor Jethro seemed to hear.

"Well . . . well . . . well," Moses stammered, something he did at times, "you don't know who I am."

It was true, Mahleendah thought. They didn't know who he was—at least she didn't. Sometimes he seemed so intelligent. Moses knew how to deal with people, especially those Amalekite shepherds who used to bother them. He knew how to negotiate for the best deals with the traders who came through with grain and food and got the best prices for the clan's wool. Yet other times he seemed discouraged, a beaten man who had lost a great battle, though she couldn't imagine anything ever defeating him. The Egyptian was a puzzling man.

"We know who you are, Moses," Jethro said softly. As he glanced up sharply, Moses's eyes met the priest's. Mahleendah crept closer to the fire, forgetting the food lying in the dust.

"You think we get no news from Egypt out here? Yet every caravan that comes through the desert this direction stops by here to trade or just to eat. We hear many things."

"What have you heard?"

"We heard of one who was in the palace and assumed to be the son of Pharaoh's daughter. Yet he refused to worship the gods of Egypt and chose to identify with the God of the Hebrews." Moses flinched as if Jethro had struck him. "We heard of a fight in which he defended a Hebrew slave against a slave master and killed the overseer. We heard that he fled from Egypt and totally disappeared and no one knows where he is. About the same time as you showed up at our well."

Moses lowered his eyes. "So are you going to return me to Egypt?"

"Don't be silly!" said Jethro, "I want you for a son. If you are good enough for the Pharaoh, you're more than good enough for the likes of me." Both men laughed nervously.

"I do worship the one God," Moses explained, "but I am a failure and a disappointment. I was to lead the one God's people out of their slavery, and yet my short temper ruined God's plan. I had to escape here to the desert where I will probably spend the rest of my life in hiding." He shrugged. "I am a failure."

Jethro listened quietly. "The one God is very wise," he said. "Often His plans are more complicated than what we understand at the time."

His reply did not comfort Moses.

"Meanwhile," Jethro continued, slapping him on the shoulder, "you have a life to live, my son. Come be my son. I will give you Zipporah, my oldest daughter. Marry her, be my heir."

Moses clasped the man's hand in his. "I will, and I will treat your daughter well."

Jethro nodded. "It's settled then. I thought I was going to have to travel elsewhere to find some God-fearing relatives for my daughters to marry. I could hardly let them marry those shepherds who pester them all the time. . . . Well," he chuckled, "who used to pester them before you came."

Moses smiled. "They won't be bothering them any time soon," he said. The two men laughed.

Mahleendah slipped backward into the darkness. *I've got to tell Zipporah,* she thought. Would Zipporah be happy? Most likely, for all of them had admired the stranger from Egypt, and yet of all of them, Zipporah was the most headstrong. Mahleendah turned and ran toward the girls' tent. She could hardly wait to share the news.

* * *

Mahleendah scampered along next to Moses. It was hard to match his long powerful strides through the wadi as he led the sheep away from the encampment toward a grazing area. "It's not going to be too much longer now," she observed to Moses, who nodded. Zipporah's baby was due any day, and she was too big and too uncomfortable to hike out with her husband and the sheep. She stayed in the shelter of the family tent. "Are you hoping for a boy or a girl?" Mahleendah asked.

Moses glanced at the girl. "I'm hoping for a healthy child," he said, "who looks like his mother."

"His mother? So you want a boy?"

He laughed. "I suppose every man wants a boy, but I would love a daughter too. Whatever the Lord sends me, I will accept."

"Yeah, that's what Father always said, but I think he wished he had a boy."

"Well, he has me."

Mahleendah laughed. When Moses wasn't busy singing depressing songs to himself out in the wilderness, he could have a real arrogant streak at times.

"Yes, what more could Father desire than an Egyptian prince for a son-in-law?"

Moses winced. "It's best we never speak of that. Besides, no Egyptian prince would ever tend sheep."

The girl was silent for a few moments, then threw back her

shoulders. "Well, I'm proud to care for the sheep of the clan of Jethro. There are a lot worse things."

Moses nodded. "Yes, there are, and we should be grateful to the one God for giving us the life He does."

The girl enjoyed tending the flocks with Moses even though he was easily distracted and spent much of his day scribbling on papyrus instead of watching the sheep. He was so interesting to talk to. She always marveled at how someone could be so intelligent about so many things and yet so ignorant about the ways of sheep. However, in the years since he had joined the clan and married her sister, Zipporah, he had learned a lot.

"What are you scribbling about this week?"

Moses looked surprised.

"Oh, don't act so surprised. We all know what you do when you're out watching the sheep."

"I . . . I . . ." Moses started to stammer, "I'm just writing the stories that your father tells me. My mother told me stories of Isaac and Jacob—the ones she knew—but your father has related to me so many more that are part of my family history, too, and I just don't want to forget them."

"Your family history?" Mahleendah demanded. "We're not related to any Egyptians."

"Someday it will all make sense to you, maybe," Moses continued. "Right now, I don't want to talk about it. But I'll tell you about the story I'm writing down. It's the one your father told us last week. The one about the wealthy man from the land of Uz."

"Oh, Job."

"Yes. It was a fascinating story, and even though he went through such difficult times during the middle of his life, our one God took good care of him and restored everything and more to him later and rewarded him for his endurance."

"He's like that," the girl said. "And He's going to do that for you, too."

Moses stared at her.

"He will," she insisted. "He's like that to those who love Him and are faithful to Him. You'll see."

"I guess it's hard to see from this point in life," he said. "Perhaps I made too many mistakes and He's put me out here in the desert with these sheep where I can't mess up His plans any worse than I already have."

Mahleendah laughed. "The one God is very kind and gracious. He's patient and forgiving and gives us second chances and third chances and prepares us other plans when we make mistakes. The God of Abraham is just and fair. While He does punish people who are bad, to those who are sorry He offers forgiveness. Maybe you should have Father sacrifice a lamb for you. You know, if you offer a sin offering, He has promised to take away any wrong things you've ever done. It's as if you never did them and the mistakes that you made are transferred onto the lamb. When it dies, your sins are paid for."

Moses watched her intently. "I will speak to Jethro about this," he said finally.

"Good. Then maybe you'll quit singing such depressing songs. I think the one God prefers us to sing happy praises to Him instead of this miserable stuff you sing about your sins always being before your face."

Her brother-in-law reddened. "You have been listening."

"Uh huh. I'm sorry for anyone who feels like that all the time, but I don't believe that our God has sent you out in the desert here to punish you for whatever it is you did. He has a plan, and you just need to be patient. Hopefully, though, it won't be one that takes you away from us. Zipporah would be very upset."

Moses laughed. "She is my wife. If the plan took me away from here, she would go with me."

Mahleendah thought a moment. "Oh, probably so. I suppose all of us will have to leave Father when we marry."

"Yes, that's usually the way it works, but when you have a husband, at least no one will make you go away from him. You can count on being with him the rest of your life."

"Well, then I hope he's a nice one and not like those pesky shepherds."

He roared with laughter. "Now, Mahleendah, those pesky shepherds haven't bothered you for several years."

"That's true, but I remember what they did before you came."

"I recall them very politely drawing all the water you needed for your sheep that day."

The girl shrieked with laughter. "Yes, they did. It made them so angry. They don't even come to this well to water their sheep anymore, which is fine by me. I'm glad you're here with us, Moses."

Although he smiled, he couldn't bring himself to say that he also was glad to be there. Mahleendah decided to change the subject.

"You know, I'm pretty well grown up now," she said. "I'm 14 now. I've been of marriageable age for years."

"Yes," he said, "you seemed like such a little girl when I joined your family."

"I'm grown up," Mahleendah insisted.

"And a fine woman you have become."

"Has Father talked to you about a husband for me?"

"Yes, Jethro has discussed making a trip back east to find some of his relatives who might still worship the one God."

"He's always said he would rather see us unmarried than coupled with someone who did not worship our God," she said, "but most of the people who worship our God are in Egypt."

"As slaves. That would hardly be the place to look for a fitting husband for you."

"Well, Father might not have to look that far for a husband for me."

"Oh? You've given this some thought?"

Now it was her turn to blush and stammer. "Well—uh—yes. You know the traders who come through here?"

"Many pass through. Which ones?"

"Well, the one that has the young man who's traveling with his uncle. Apparently his parents have died. They were metalworkers."

"Ah, yes. But I don't believe his relatives worship the one God."

"That's true, but Keenan does."

"Keenan," Moses echoed. "H'mm, you know this young man's name?"

"Well, I just picked it up in passing," the girl stammered.

"Just in passing, huh?" he teased. "How is it that he's a worshiper of the one God when his uncle wears amulets to several other deities?"

"His parents were," she said.

"It is difficult for a young man to stay loyal to the God of his parents when all those he lives with worship other gods," Moses agreed. "Perhaps I can speak to Jethro about this, and we can invite him to stay in our camp until his uncle comes through on his next journey. We could use some better metal implements—knives and other things. That will give your father and I a chance to get to know him."

"Oh, thank you," Mahleendah beamed, then she rushed off to chase a wayward sheep.

SENEFRU

he transition from being a recorder for Mahleendah and my next human was a simple one. I love it when the Almighty provides me with such continuity between my assignments. Mahleendah married her metalworker, Keenan, and moved to Egypt where there was more metalwork available. Keenan set up a shop and has done quite well.

Senefru stood and stretched his back. Perspiration poured from him and he was glad for the light headdress that protected him from the sun.

"Time to switch places," his father grunted. The boy nodded thankfully and moved over to the bellows. Placing his foot on them, he started pumping as his father bent over the forge, watching for the copper ingots to melt so he could pour the metal in the clay molds.

"This is hard work," Senefru said more to himself than his father.

Keenan paused and eyed his son. "Yes, it is hard work, but it could be a lot worse."

The boy wiped his forehead. "Hotter than this?"

His father shook his head. "No, probably not, but we are free men. We could be slaves. Their lives are worse, and I'm sure they're just as hot laboring in the brickyards, in the fields, and on the building projects."

Senefru sighed. It was true. At least when he and his father did their work no one stood over them with a whip. He had grown up in Egypt, so unless someone pointed them out, he tended to ignore the slaves and their plight. His father was a man of few words but seemed more interested in the slaves than a normal Egyptian should. The boy shrugged. Most of his friends mentioned little things about their fathers that embarrassed them too.

As if able to read his thoughts, his father looked him in the eye and said, "They're people, too, you know."

Embarrassed, Senefru stared at his feet. "Who do you mean?"

"You know who I mean—and they are people too. Someday they will be free, and when that happens the few that have been kind to them will be glad they were."

The boy eyed the bent, scarred backs of the brickmakers slowly dragging their loads past them and shook his head. He was pretty sure slaves didn't have the same kinds of feelings as normal people. They certainly didn't seem to, anyway. At any rate, it wasn't his problem, and he planned to have as little to do with them as possible. Perhaps being the son of a metal smith wasn't so bad after all.

* * *

There was something different about today. Although Senefru could not put his finger on what it was, yet he could feel it in his bones. At breakfast his mother had seemed excited or uptight, he wasn't sure which. She and his father conversed in low tones for a few moments before they left.

"Is something important happening?" he asked his father as they walked toward the street of the metal workers.

"Things may be changing soon, you'll see."

"What kinds of things?"

His father mumbled something.

"What does that mean?" his son asked.

"It's best that we not talk about it right now."

Senefru kicked a rock. Typical! Here he was practically a man, but no one would tell him anything. All of the metalworkers had their shops in an area near the building projects. Since the Pharaoh was their biggest customer and owned and supplied all the raw materials, it made sense to work where it was most convenient for him and his projects.

Egyptians operated the shop next to Keenan's. The owners had some of the Hebrew slaves there working for them. Senefru secretly hoped that someday he and his father would be doing well enough financially to buy a few slaves. It would certainly lighten his load.

Today Father was acting strangely. When the shop next to them stopped for their midmorning break and the slaves went over to the goatskin bag of water hanging on the wall, Father paused near them. Even though he was facing in a different direction, he seemed to be whispering to them.

Senefru casually sauntered by to see if he could hear what they were talking about. "Yes," Oholiab, one of the slaves, said almost inaudibly, "he is here. Came last night. He is staying in the house of Aaron. Too bad his parents have died." More whispering.

Senefru headed back to his shop to overhear more of the conversation. "Yes, his two sons are with him. His wife, I understand, came part way with him, then she returned to Midian."

The boy's ears perked up. How did his father have anything to do with slaves?

It wasn't difficult for me to figure out what Keenan and the slaves were talking about, but then I knew who was back in Egypt. I had seen his guardian the previous night.

That afternoon the scribe who was Keenan's contact for business strode into their shop. Keenan put his hammer stone down. "Let's take a break for minute," he said to his son.

Senefru was only too happy to comply. He removed his foot from the bellows and stretched his aching back.

"What is the commotion at the palace?" Keenan asked his visitor.

The scribe laughed. "Such excitement you're missing today. I'm glad I don't work at a job like yours."

Senefru bristled at the comment but one sharp look from his

father reminded him to keep silent at least until the man had left.

"You wouldn't believe who has come back to town," the man continued. "You remember the stories of Moses? I must admit I was a child when all that happened, but it was hot news. He was our military leader and considered the son of the pharaoh or at least of pharaoh's daughter. Everyone thought he would be the next pharaoh when the old king died. Then he started hanging around the slaves, and next thing you know he was taking their side against the overseers—at least that's what I heard. Apparently he killed one. That's bad for discipline. You start having someone take their side, and pretty soon you can't get any of them to obey. It's bad for discipline all over. He wasn't doing the country any favors. Pharaoh knew it. That's why he got rid of him, or Moses ran away or something.

"Anyway, he's back in town after 40 years. Perhaps he thought we'd forgotten who he was by now. Strange, he doesn't look as old as he must be. Strode right into the palace as if he hadn't been gone a week and acted as if he owned the place." The chatty Egyptian shook his head. "It was as if he hadn't left. Now he just walked right in, interrupted the court proceedings, and announced to the pharaoh it was time to let all the slaves go free—at least all the Hebrew slaves."

"Free?" the boy's father asked.

"Well, not exactly," the Egyptian backpedaled. "He said—let's see—something about letting them all go out in the desert to make a sacrifice to their God. As if any king in his right mind is going to let an entire population of slaves run off in the middle of the desert somewhere to worship a God that isn't even a proper Egyptian deity." He laughed and then stopped when he realized he was the only one seeing anything amusing.

"What did the pharaoh say?" Keenan asked.

"Well, he said no, of course, but what was really amazing was that this Moses fellow had the gall to threaten him."

"He threatened the pharaoh?" Senefru blurted.

"Yes, young one. Did a couple magic tricks that our magicians duplicated, then told him his God was going to do bad things to the pharaoh if he didn't let them go. The nerve of him! Of course, nothing happened, and we all laughed at him, but it amazes me that he had the nerve to do it."

"Did the pharaoh do anything about him?" Keenan questioned, looking worried.

"Not a thing. He figures all those years out with the sand dwellers have affected his mind. Besides, he was a part of the royal family at one time, so I suppose they're dealing gently with him. They just let him go. He may be insane but he seems harmless."

Senefru wondered if the incident could have anything to do with his father's whispered conversation with Oholiab, the slave from the next metal shop. Was this part of the mysterious discussion between his parents?

"Anyway," the scribe continued, "I came to pick up those knives that we ordered last week and to let you know about how many spear tips we are going to need. They have just recruited a new batch of Nubians, so we'll be needing to equip them."

Keenan brought the knives.

"Meanwhile, keep an eye out for that Moses fellow," the scribe added. "He's a harmless idiot, but the pharaoh doesn't want him hurt, I suppose out of respect for what he used to be."

As the man left, Senefru turned to his father. "So we have one more crazy old man in town." His father just gave him a strange look.

"There's nothing crazy about Moses," Keenan said finally, "and if the pharaoh is smart, he'll remember that soon."

"You know something about this man? Tell me! Did you run into him in the desert when you traveled with the merchant caravans?"

"You might say that, but the less said the better. Come on, we've got spearheads to cast."

"But, Father," Senefru protested.

His father's jaw was set. "Get pumping those bellows, son. This fire isn't hot enough to melt a thing."

Senefru returned to working the bellows to heat up the coals. "I don't know why we have to do this part of the work ourselves," he mumbled to himself. "If we had slaves like the other metal workers, we could let them handle this part of the job." He frequently felt jealous of Bezaleel and Oholiab. No matter how hard he and his father worked and how perfect their instruments and bowls and knives turned out, they never looked as good next to their neighbors' wares. The slaves worked with gold and even that rarest of all metals in Egypt, silver.

Again and again his father had told him not to be envious. "Pharaoh is going to use a lot more bronze spear tips than they will golden bowls. The money is in the items that have the most demand. We're in the right business." Senefru sighed. It might be true but he still wished he worked in the next shop.

That evening, instead of stretching out and relaxing after supper, his father motioned to him. "Get your cloak, Senefru."

"Where are we going?" But his mother and father had both pulled on their outer cloaks and started out the door. He followed quickly. As they left the familiar part of town his suspicion started rising.

"Where are we going?" he asked his father again. "Are you sure you know the right place? We're heading right for the slave quarters."

"Hush," his father said. "You must not speak unless we are alone. Just keep your eyes and ears open. You'll understand in time."

Senefru grudgingly did as he was told. His eyes widened as he walked into the slave district. He wasn't sure it was even safe to be here. What was Father thinking? Then his parents turned into a small alley and knocked on a door. The three of them heard a muffled response. "It is Keenan," his father announced, "son-in-law of Jethro, priest of Midian."

Priest of where? Senefru wondered. Son-in-law? Did that mean this Jethro person was his grandfather, mother's father? The door opened and an elderly slave woman stood before them, but Mother rushed past her and hugged the two boys standing in the corner.

Senefru stared in amazement. Who were these people? Then as if his father had heard his thoughts out loud, he said, "Senefru, these are your cousins." The boy stared at the young men. "Their names are Gershom and Eliezer, " Father continued. His son studied the two strangers. Gershom was definitely older than he was, while Eliezer was closer to his age.

"I understand why you came here last night when you arrived," Senefru's mother said, "but wouldn't you be more comfortable staying at our place? And why didn't your mother come with you?"

"Father sent her back home," Gershom explained. "He said she would not be happy when the plagues came. Our father always says our mother has a sensitive nature. He says that we will have to leave before long, too."

"Plagues?" Senefru repeated, puzzled.

Then his father spoke. "This will work out well. We have just received an order from the pharaoh for new spearheads, and we could use an extra couple pairs of hands. Gershom and Eliezer can help us in our shop."

Senefru shook his head. His father was trying to be diplomatic to the slaves again. Why did he bother?

"This will work out well," Keenan repeated. "You boys will work with me, but we must not speak of this. It is critically important that no one find out that you are the sons of Moses."

Senefru's mouth dropped open. The sons of Moses? The Moses who had just threatened Pharaoh that morning? Was it safe to be associated with him in any way? Apparently Father hadn't thought about that, for the two boys quickly gathered up their few belongings and headed out of the tiny slave dwelling

* * *

It was good to have two more pairs of hands in the metalworking shop, even if they were inexperienced ones. Senefru's father obtained a second set of bellows and additional blowpipes to heat the metalworking fires. Gershom and Eliezer were able to pump the bellows or use the blowpipes with very little training, while Senefru and his father poured the molten bronze into the clay spearhead molds. Gershom was fascinated with the goldsmiths next door.

"What are they doing?" he questioned. "They aren't doing things the same way we do."

"Of course not," Senefru scoffed. "They're working with gold."

"It's more beautiful than copper or bronze," Gershom observed.

Senefru nodded. "They can beat gold into a really thin layer they call gold leaf. Then they put it on statues and furniture and the insides of buildings."

"I've heard of such things," Gershom said, "but I've never seen it."

"Keep those bellows going, boys," Father declared. "I don't mind you talking, but you can't stop pumping."

I smiled to myself. With so many new things to look at, it's no wonder they were distracted.

Suddenly a man stumbled into the metalworkers' quarter, dripping with sweat and looking frightened. "The Nile is bleeding," he gasped. Work came to an abrupt halt as everyone gathered around the distraught individual.

"The Nile—I think it's dying." He struggled to get the words out. "When Pharaoh went down to the river this morning to praise Hapy, as he does every morning, Moses was there to meet him."

"Moses? Who is Moses?" interrupted one metalworker.

"You know," another responded, "the crazy man who wants Pharaoh to allow all the Hebrew slaves go out in the desert." Senefru glanced at Eliezer, but the boy kept his eyes firmly fixed on the toe of his sandal.

"Anyway," the first man continued after catching his breath, "this Moses was standing there at the river, and he struck the water with his rod, and it turned into blood, and the whole river has become blood."

"Can it be true?" someone asked. "Let's go see."

"May we go, Father?" Senefru said.

"No, we have plenty of work to do. If it's true, we'll find out soon enough. Now get back to work." Silently the boys returned to their duties. But it seemed only minutes before word came back that blood filled the entire Nile. Not just colored water; it smelled terrible and was undrinkable.

"What are we going to do?" Senefru questioned his father.

"Nothing. It isn't our problem. This is between Moses and Pharaoh and all his magicians. We have work to do." He continued to break open the spearhead molds. Then he took the tongs he had been using to handle the hot objects and stuck them in a water vat to cool them down. They made their usual hiss and steam. Suddenly Keenan cried out in shock. The boys dropped what they were doing and rushed to see what was wrong. Even the water in the vat had turned to blood, and the tongs had a strange crust on them. A familiar stench filled the air.

"Dried blood?" Senefru asked.

Unable to speak, Keenan nodded. The boys stared at the tongs.

"Let's go home," Keenan sighed. "We can't continue without water."

They silently went through the duties of shutting down the workshop and headed for home. The streets were filled with workers unable to finish what they were doing. Everyone was talking about the water.

"It's not just the Nile," someone commented. "The irrigation canals and even the water in our drinking jars and buckets are full of blood." Panic seemed to linger just below the surface.

"What are we going to do?" everyone asked.

When the four men reached their home they found Mother working in the shade in the yard. "Have you heard?" Keenan asked.

She nodded. "Yes, and we have also heard that Pharaoh has called his counselors to the palace to find out how to deal with the situation."

"Well," her husband replied, "we can't just sit around. I think the boys and I will go down near the Nile and try digging a well or at least a small hole close by and see if we can get fresh water that way."

The boys groaned. It had almost sounded as if they might have an afternoon off. Reluctantly, they picked up wooden shovels and digging sticks and followed Keenan toward the river.

Senefru and his father returned with two small leather buckets of water that they had painstakingly scooped from a little hole by the Nile. Mother had just returned from the marketplace with some food for supper.

"We have some water, Mother," Senefru said, holding up the bucket, "but not very much. It doesn't look all that clean. You may want to pour it through a cloth or something a couple times, but it's better than what's flowing down the Nile."

"Thank you, boys. I'm glad that the Lord left a way for us still to get a little water, or we would all die before we ever left this place."

"Left this place?" Senefru sputtered.

"We're not going anywhere," Keenan interrupted. "I'm sure your mother didn't mean to say that."

"My mistake," Mother said. "Anyway, there's news in the market from Pharaoh. Apparently the wise men were also able to turn water into blood at the palace, so Pharaoh believes this is just a trick."

"What a powerful piece of magic," Senefru exclaimed, turning to Gershom and Eliezer. "Does your father do stuff like this at home too?"

They stared at each other. "No," they said, "never."

"Well, it's still really great," Senefru protested. "He must have the heart of a lion, being able to stand up to Pharaoh like that."

Gershom and Eliezer glanced at each other again with that same awkward look.

Senefru sensed something going on between them. "What is it?" he blurted.

Moses' sons awkwardly shuffled their feet and stared at the ground, then Gershom cleared his throat. "Actually, Father is usually kind of shy. He doesn't talk much, because—well, when he's nervous he tends to stutter a bit."

"Then do you think that he's sort of gone a little crazy?" Senefru demanded without thinking.

Moses' sons at first remained silent, then Gershom said, "The one God sent him here to Egypt. He never wanted to return to this horrible place."

"Horrible place?" Senefru echoed.

"It's not that horrible," his mother interrupted. "We have a pretty good life here."

"Well, of course you do," Gershom replied. "You're free—but look how the Hebrews are treated."

"So?" Senefru demanded. "Probably anywhere you go you will find rich people and their slaves."

"But these are Father's people," Gershom explained patiently. "He's a Hebrew."

Confused, Senefru frowned to himself. His cousins were from Midian, so he assumed that they were Midianites, though they said that they were descended from Abraham. However, they were from Abraham's second wife Keturah and his sons, not through Issac, the "promised one."

"Well," Gershom continued, "the God of the Hebrews, whom my grandfather also worships, has chosen Moses to lead them out of Egypt and slavery. The Only One wants to make the great nation that he promised Abraham a long time ago. Moses is just here doing what the one God told him to."

"Why do you keep calling him the one God?" Senefru asked. "There are hundreds of Gods here in Egypt—the great ones Pharaoh serves, and the lesser ones the ordinary people worship—but still lots of them. So who's this one God, and doesn't He have a name?"

"He tells Moses His name is 'I am.'"

"'I am?'" Senefru frowned again. This God was as confusing as his uncle Moses. The boy would stick with the familiar Egyptian gods. It just made more sense.

* * *

A week had gone by. Every day the boys spent several hours digging in the soft clay by the river, trying to scoop what brackish water they could into their buckets. They had barely enough for drinking and cooking and everything in the metalwork shop had come to a standstill. It wasn't just their shop. All of Egypt suffered from the drinking water shortage.

A neighbor woman slipped into their courtyard and motioned to Senefru's mother. Quickly the two women slipped out toward the marketplace. The boys, who had just gotten back from finding water, followed them. What were the women up to?

Through the marketplace strode an old slave and another individual who carried himself in a manner that told Senefru he was not a slave although he resembled the other man. Murmurs rippled through the crowd. "It's Moses and Aaron. They're on their way to the palace."

"Who's the slave with him? Is that Moses' slave?" someone asked.

"No, he speaks for Moses. Moses makes the decisions, and the slave communicates to everyone else what he has decided."

Senefru's forehead wrinkled in thought. So this was the father of Gershom and Eliezer. How would his one God hold up against the gods of Egypt? Nothing was stronger than its deities. They had made Egypt a powerful nation. Yet, apparently, the one God had been stronger than Pharaoh (Horus incarnate on earth), who was responsible for the flow of the Nile and insured that it kept the fields fertile. The one God had made it flow blood and death instead of bringing life. Would the Hebrew be more powerful than the others, too?

They waited outside Pharaoh's palace, eagerly straining to get any news rippling back through the crowd.

"Frogs, we're going to have frogs," someone announced.

The people started to laugh. "Frogs?"

"This is a curse? That's no problem. We worship Heket, who manifests herself as a frog. She is the protector of unborn babies."

Obviously the one God didn't know how Egyptians felt about frogs. "We think frogs are great," Senefru laughed. "We wouldn't hurt frogs, and we don't mind them being around. Besides, they eat bugs. Frogs are great! That curse from your God isn't going to bother anyone here," he said to Eliezer.

The other boy looked at his sandals. "What's a frog? I don't think we have many of those where we live."

"You probably don't. Let's go back down to the river where we were digging for water, and I'll show you. They're really harmless."

As the crowd dispersed, laughing, the boys turned and headed back toward the bleeding Nile in search of frogs.

* * *

A piercing scream shattered the air and in seconds Senefru was awake and on his feet. He reached for his loincloth and ran out into the courtyard. "What is it, Mother?" he shouted. As he stepped into the courtyard he felt a sickening squish under his foot, then slid and fell.

"Oh, that's disgusting," he said. Kicking the crushed frog out of the way, he jumped back up to see what had frightened his mother so much.

She was now just standing wordless in the courtyard. Then he saw them—frogs everywhere. They were hopping around in her kneading trough and on the oven in which she baked the family's bread every morning. When she opened the grain basket to grind some more flour, frogs leaped out of it.

"What are we gonna do?" she asked. "I can't stand this."

"Don't be disrespectful," her husband whispered. "You don't want to offend Heket. She might not protect you if you have another childbirth."

"I stepped on one and squashed it flat—you never saw such a mess," Senefru interrupted.

"Hush," his father hissed. "Now we're going to have to offer sacrifices to Heket. You mustn't kill them."

"I didn't mean to—I didn't even see it."

"From now on we have to be very careful," his father said. "We can't act as if we don't like them. They're sacred here."

"I just can't stand it," Mahleendah repeated, hysteria in her voice. "I can't have frogs in my grain basket."

Keenan shook his head. "I wonder if it's this bad everywhere else. I'm going down to the shop and see what's happening there."

"We'll come with you," his cousins, who had all gotten their clothes on by now, volunteered.

"Don't you want some bread before you go?" Senefru's mother asked as she shooed the frogs off the top of it.

"Uh . . . no thanks, Mother."

Gershom and Eliezer shook their heads. "We're not very hungry this morning, but thank you anyway."

Her shoulders sagged. "I wouldn't eat it either. Forget it."

They scurried out the gate and found it was no better in the street. All through town families were having the same crisis.

Should they shoo the frogs out of their houses? Would it offend Heket? Or should they feel honored that frogs filled the land? And where did they all come from?

The marketplace was the place to go to get the latest news. Apparently Pharaoh had gone down to the Nile early to offer his daily devotions. It was a little embarrassing to have other people seeing him still doing it with the Nile still flowing red.

Moses and Aaron had met him at the river's edge. There Moses had whispered something to Aaron and had held his hand out toward the Nile—and the frogs came pouring out. Within minutes they had spread all through the town.

"Yes, but the funniest thing was," said a little man who had everyone's attention, "Pharaoh turned to his priests and advisors and asked if they could do it too. They held their hands out, and frogs poured from their sleeves. That's just what we needed—more frogs!" The crowd roared with laughter.

Gershom smirked. "I guess the one God figures that if you consider frogs sacred, He'll give you the desires of your heart. You should have enough frogs for everyone to have their own to worship here."

"And more," Senefru groaned. "But this is ridiculous! No one is going to be able to get anything done with all these frogs in the way. I wonder if they've invaded the palace."

"Oh, yes," responded a palace slave at the market to do some trading. "And it's as upsetting to them as it is to the rest of us, only the pharaoh is insisting it's just a trick and he doesn't mind it at all. He has announced that frogs are welcome in Egypt."

"Frogs have always been welcome in Egypt," one man grumbled. "We just never expected to have quite this many."

"It looks as if the God of Moses is stronger than Pharaoh and Heket," Gershom commented.

"Nonsense," the little man in the market snapped. "If anything, Heket is greater than the God of Moses, and she's showing her strength by filling the land with her representatives. The God of Moses has no power. Pharaoh will hold strong. And who are you, young man, with your foreign accent?" Senefru pulled him away before there was any trouble. They pushed their way through the crowd and started for home.

The sun was getting high in the sky and the boys were starting to get very hungry since they had skipped breakfast. They hoped that Senefru's mother would figure out some way to prepare the midday meal, preferably a frog-free one.

By that night even Pharaoh had changed his mind. It was possible to have too many frogs. A contingent of the royal guard went to the slave quarters of town to request the presence of Moses and Aaron. The rumor was that Pharaoh had agreed to let all the Hebrew slaves go into the desert to worship their God if He would just get rid of the frogs. Senefru and his cousins followed the guards back to the palace.

"So that you won't think that the frogs died of natural causes," Moses declared, "you may choose the time that you want all of them to leave, and the one God will do it then."

"Tomorrow morning," Pharaoh replied, "at dawn."

"So let it be. Tomorrow morning at dawn the one God will rid the land of frogs except for those who live in the river." He and Aaron turned and left the palace.

"Do you think they'll all really die at once?" Senefru asked his cousins when they learned what had happened. "How can your father do that?"

"Yes, I think they will," Eliezer said. "The one God created everything, so He can withdraw life from anything He wants to all at once or one at a time. Whatever it is He says He will do, He can."

Senefru shook his head. It sounded a little far-fetched to him, but then lately a lot of things were happening that he had never thought he would see.

The next morning it was just as Moses had declared. The frogs still covered Egypt, but they were dead. They lay everywhere, their bodies drying out in the sun, their bulging eyeballs sinking into their heads as they withered. Flies buzzed everywhere, and the smell was terrible.

Senefru's parents had a heated but whispered argument. Even though they tried to talk quietly, the boys could hear the whole thing.

"I don't care," Mother hissed. "We are not Egyptians, have never worshiped Heket, and I'm not about to start now! I'm not having dead frogs all over my house! I'm going to get rid of them."

"You mustn't do that," her husband protested. "It might be a sign of disrespect to Heket."

"Well, I'd say that the one God has already shown such disrespect that a little more from me won't even be noticed," she snapped. "And I'm not having dead frogs lying all over the house. You can either help me or get out of the way!" Folding her arms, she waited for him to reply.

Keenan pushed past and disappeared down the street.

"Come on, boys," Mother said. "Give us a hand here. This is disgusting!" They gathered up baskets of frogs. She made them dig a hole in the courtyard and dump all the frogs in it and cover them with dirt.

"I see no reason to act like Egyptians when we aren't," Senefru's mother explained as they worked. "It's one thing to fit in, but when it involves having dead frogs lying all over the place—that's just asking a little too much of me."

"I bet we'll hear more of that before this is over," Gershom mumbled. "This plan of the one God certainly isn't good for our relationships with the Egyptians."

"Ouch!" Senefru suddenly yelped, slapping at an insect biting the back of his neck. "Where did these all come from?"

"I don't know," Gershom replied. "They're all over the place. Ow!" He slapped at another one. The cow in the courtyard kept twitching and flicking her tail. "Look, they're biting her, too," he said, running his hand over her side.

"I've never seen so many of these little things at once, even for this time of year," Senefru commented with surprise. "You don't suppose your father is involved with this, do you?"

His cousins both shrugged. "We don't really know what he is up to, and hear things only in the marketplace just as you do," Gershom said, a wistful tone in his voice.

Senefru stopped and thought about it for a moment. "I hope this isn't another plague," he said finally. "If it is, it means that Pharaoh changed his mind and decided that all those frogs just died spontaneously. Of course," he added after thinking for a moment, "I guess they would if they got that far away from water. Frogs need to be near the river to live."

"Oh, stop it," Gershom exploded. "You're as bad as Pharaoh. How much is it going to take to convince you that the one God is more powerful than the other gods of Egypt?"

"I don't know. I'm not convinced yet. But I sure wish—ouch!— these things would quit biting."

The cow mooed in agreement.

"Well," Gershom added, "I wish He could convince you without these things biting me and without me having to deal with dead frogs and stinking water. It would be much more fair if God picked on only the people who didn't believe in Him."

"Maybe your God doesn't know how to do that," Senefru sighed.

Eliezer snorted. "The one God could do anything He wants to— He just hasn't chosen to. If He did, He could make all of the plagues happen just to the Egyptians."

"Well, why don't you ask Him to?" Senefru said. "Maybe Moses isn't the only one He listens to."

The boys stared at each other. "No one speaks face to face to the one God and lives," Gershom explained.

"Well," Senefru replied, "your father looks pretty alive to me. Old, but extremely active for a man in his eighties."

The boys laughed. "Yes, our father has spoken with God," Gershom said, "and God has spoken with him. They just don't do it face to face. God speaks to him through burning bushes, in his mind, and things like that."

"Well, it all sounds weird to me, but don't you just pray to Him like we do to our gods?"

Gershom pulled himself up to his full height. "Yes, and I'm going to."

The boys were right. The biting insects were another plague. Only this time Pharaoh's magicians and wise men were not able to produce more gnats.

"Well, we can be thankful for that," Senefru commented when he heard about it. "That's just what we don't need—more gnats."

"Ah," said an old man in the marketplace, "but it means that the magicians have now bowed to the one God. He can do something they can't do."

The smile vanished from Senefru's face. *It did mean that,* he thought. Still he wasn't certain. "So what happens now?"

"Well," continued the old man, "Moses and Aaron were up early this morning. They surprised Pharaoh as he was going down to the river. I hear that the message from the one God was 'If you don't let My people go, I will send large numbers of flies. I will inflict them on you and your officials and on all your people and into your homes. Then the houses of the Egyptians will be full of flies. But the area of Goshen will be different. That's where my people live. There will not be large numbers of flies in Goshen. Then you will know that I, the Lord, am in this land. I will treat My people differently from yours. This miraculous sign will take place tomorrow.'"

Senefru stared at the old man. "How long ago was that?"

"Oh, about an hour."

Senefru looked around and saw flies in the marketplace. But there always were.

As they headed toward home with the newest news, Gershom nudged Senefru. "Did you hear it? The one God answered my prayer. He's going to treat the Hebrews differently."

His cousin's jaw dropped. It was true. If the message the old man in the marketplace told was accurate, God was going to protect those who believed in Him. He felt a prickling sensation along his spine. Just how powerful was this God of Moses? Perhaps he needed to rethink a few things. A buzzing that seemed to get louder and louder cut short his musings. "There are an awful lot of flies here today," he said.

"Yes," Gershom replied cheerfully, "a whole lot more than there were a half hour ago."

"What do you sound so happy about? I hate flies, and we don't live in Goshen. That's the smelly slave part of town."

Eliezer laughed. "Smelly? This whole place still smells like dead frogs to me."

Senefru shot him a sharp glance. It was true. The Egyptians had respectfully moved the rotting frog corpses and stacked them into piles so that they could at least walk on the streets without stepping on them and causing more desecration. The whole city reeked. Senefru looked around. Flies covered the piles. The insects didn't seem to have much respect for Heket's representatives. Another swarm of them started buzzing around Senefru's head. He swatted at them.

"These are getting really annoying," he complained, then started to cough and choke.

Gershom and Eliezer convulsed with laughter as Senefru finally coughed out the offending fly and spat it on the ground.

"Thanks a lot," he growled.

"I think it's going to get worse before it gets better," Eliezer announced pleasantly. And it did.

* * *

Senefru took one look at his mother's tear-streaked face and knew it had happened. "Oh, Mother," he said, putting his arms around her. She laid her head on his shoulder and sobbed.

"I told your father this would happen. I told him we should take the cow over to the land of Goshen and let her stay with Moses' family, at least while the cattle plague was going on. But he thinks it would be really bad for business if it appeared we were siding with the Hebrews. And now she is dead. And it's not just that we won't have milk or cheese, but she and I were kind of friends, too."

"I know," said Senefru, hugging her tightly. "Do you know what happened?"

"No. I stood out there with her, telling her it was going to be alright. And then she just shuddered and died."

"Do you think it would be safe to butcher her for meat?"

"No. From what I've heard in the marketplace, the Lord said it was a plague that all the animals would die from. I don't know what kind of plague He meant, but whatever it is, it's diseased meat, and I don't think it would be safe to eat it."

Senefru frowned. "Probably not. Why don't you go somewhere else for a while? I'll find Gershom and Eliezer and see if we can't remove her."

"Where are you going to take her?"

"I'm not sure, but we can't just leave her here."

Mother raised her tear-filled eyes to meet his gaze. "Everyone's cattle just died. All of the pharaoh's horses and donkeys. I don't think there's an animal left."

"What about the Israelites?" Senefru asked. "Did anything happen to their animals?"

"I don't know. In the marketplace I heard about everyone else's, and it's filled with dead animals. And the royal stables. I don't know what they're going to do to get rid of all of them. And they thought it smelled bad during the frog invasion."

Her son nodded. "This would be worse." Then he thought of something else. "Mom, do you believe in the one God?"

"I don't know. When I was a little girl, my father was a priest for the one God, and he taught us about the one God, and I believed in Him back then. One of the reasons I married your father was because he believed in the one God. It's just that when we came to Egypt it was hard to get business and it was a lot easier when we fit in with everyone else and acted like Egyptians. We just sort of stopped worshiping Him, and it's been such a long time. I never really worshiped the gods here in Egypt either. I guess I just haven't worshiped anyone."

"What about Aunt Zipporah—Gershom's and Eliezer's mother?"

"She believes in the one God. As descendants of Abraham, our people started out worshiping the one God, then most of them drifted to other gods. But my family remained faithful."

* * *

Senefru met Gershom and Eliezer coming back to the house. "Not a single one?" he asked in disbelief.

"Not a single one died," Gershom replied. "Down to the tiniest calf, every animal in the Hebrew quarter is alive and well and noisy."

"Our cow is dead," Senefru said, shaking his head.

Gershom and Eliezer looked at each other. "Why wouldn't your father let us take her to the Hebrew quarter?" Gershom asked.

"You know why," Senefru answered dejectedly.

The two boys nodded. "We talked to our father. He said everyone in Egypt is going to have to make a choice. Also he wants us to return home to Midian, where he says we'll be safer."

"Will you?"

"Yes," they said in unison. "The plagues are going to get worse, and it will be best if we wait them out with Mother."

Senefru hung his head for a minute. "I'll miss you," he sighed.

"What about you, Senefru?" Gershom continued. "Why don't you come with us? You see what's happening here. Every time the pharaoh changes his mind and decides not to let the Hebrews leave, another terrible thing happens to all of Egypt. You would be safe there. Do you really want to be part of Egypt during this battle?"

"It is the battle of the gods, isn't it?" Senefru observed.

"Yes, it is. And Egypt is losing. According to Father things are going to become even worse. He says the one God told him to tell Pharaoh that the Hebrews are His firstborn son. You know the Pharaoh considers himself—

"I know—the firstborn son of Egypt, son of Horus."

"The gods are battling it out and eventually someone's going to die. And my bet is that it's going to be the firstborn son of Egypt."

Senefru looked around rapidly. "Don't say that too loud out here."

"Well, that's what we think anyway," Eliezer added. "Come with us."

"I don't know. I must talk with my mother. I can't leave her right now. She's too upset."

"Maybe she would come with us, too," Gershom suggested. "Try to talk her into it."

"I don't think it will do any good," Senefru mumbled to himself.

* * *

Senefru awakened with a groan. His skin felt on fire and his head ached. He had never felt so terrible in his young life. When he opened his eyes and stared at his body he saw that he was covered by huge red welts that were getting bigger by the minute. They were everywhere—and they hurt.

"Mother" he called. "Mother."

When he received no answer, he went to look for her. He found his mother still lying on her sleeping mat. She, too, had the big welts—just as he had.

"Oh, I hurt so bad," she moaned.

"Me too. You've got the red things on you, too."

"They look like boils. I had one once when I was a little girl. But they're everywhere. Kind of like a story my father used to tell us when we were little girls about a prince named Job."

"Did Job die from his?" her son asked.

She smiled weakly. "No, the Lord healed him."

"Which Lord? Maybe we should offer a sacrifice to Him."

Mother looked at him for several minutes. "Probably so," she said, finally. "It was the God of Abraham."

"Of course, this is another plague. I bet everybody in Egypt has these."

"Maybe not everyone," she groaned, wincing from the pain. "I'll wager that new cow that your father bought from one of the Hebrew slaves that none of the Hebrews are afflicted with them."

"Mother, we must go there. You used to worship the one God. He might take you back. Gershom said that his father told him that the one God will accept anyone who decides to follow Him."

She looked at him with dimmed eyes. "Don't you think it's a little late for that?"

"No, Mother, you and I are still alive."

"I don't think I can walk that far—I don't think I can even stand up."

"If I can find a way for us to get there, will you come?"

"Yes," she said slowly, hesitantly.

Just then the gate opened and Keenan entered the courtyard. Although he walked with the help of a large stick, he still staggered.

"Father," Senefru exclaimed, "you're sick too?"

"Everyone in Egypt is," he said dejectedly.

"Mother and I want to go to Goshen. We believe that it's probably safe there. We think that we want to follow the one God."

"I'm not surprised," Keenan said. "He is the God of your mother's people."

"Won't you come with us?"

"Could be bad for business."

"But there is no business," Senefru protested. "We've been using up what little resources we had saved. You spent a lot of it on the new cow."

"But it's a Hebrew cow—she'll be fine."

"Maybe not, now that she belongs to us. I believe the one God is going to win and that we need to give up on the gods of Egypt."

"Take your mother," Keenan suggested, "and stay at your Aunt Miriam's for awhile. I'll be in touch and be back for you soon."

Senefru flung his arms around his father. They hugged each other fiercely and quietly for a moment, then the boy helped his mother up to go to Goshen.

* * *

Senefru let out a big sigh. It had been hard to swallow his pride and head for the slaves' part of town—even harder to ask Aunt Miriam if he could stay with her. But there they were. She had made poultices of healing herbs to put on his boils. He and his mother were resting comfortably when another slave burst into the one-room dwelling.

"Everybody needs to bring their animals inside," the man announced. "There's going to be a terrible storm."

"A storm?" Mother echoed.

"Pharaoh's wise men are too miserable with the boils to even be in the court and give him advice, and yet he's still stubbornly refusing to obey God—or at least obey Moses. Now Moses says there will be a huge storm with fire and hail and lightening and anything that remains outside will be killed. Moses says it's going to be the worst hailstorm in the entire history of Egypt."

"Well, then we need to do what he commanded," Aunt Miriam said. "Let's get the few cattle and geese indoors."

"What about my father?" Senefru asked. "Do you think he's heard about the storm?"

"I'm pretty sure he has," his mother replied. "Word races everywhere these days, especially considering how the other plagues have turned out. I'm sure that he'll be informed and will take cover. I just hope he takes the new cow in."

"But Father said that because he had bought the cow from the Hebrews, she was a Hebrew cow and it wouldn't get hurt in a plague. Do you think that's true?"

Aunt Miriam snorted. "It'll still get hurt if he doesn't take it inside like God said to."

Senefru and his mother looked at each other, but there was nothing they could do. They were too weak to walk back home and check on Keenan. He would have to make his own choices.

It wasn't long before the storm struck. It was the most frightening thing Senefru had ever lived through. Hail smashed everything, and lightening flashed back and forth. It hit tall monuments and buildings and set wooden structures on fire. Senefru, Mother, and Aunt Miriam stood clustered in the doorway, watching the storm destroy Egypt. The hail tore the leaves off the trees, flattened the grain fields, and smashed the mud brick houses. The roar of the hailstones was deafening. And the only place it didn't hail was the area of Goshen where the slaves lived.

Senefru knew how stubborn Pharaoh had been and how he had increased the workload on the slaves every time another plague struck. Would he still resist the Hebrew God? Surely not. The boy limped back to the pallet and lay down, trying to find a position that wouldn't irritate any of his still sore, but now healing, boils.

All of a sudden there was silence.

"It must be over," his mother sighed.

Closing his eyes, Senefru fell into a deep sleep.

A slave burst into the room. "He's done it again," the man announced.

Senefru sat up. "Who's done what again?"

"Pharaoh. Moses went to the palace because the king sent for him. When Moses got there Pharaoh told him, 'This time I have sinned. The Lord has done what is right and I and my people were wrong. Please pray to your God. We've had enough thunder and hail. I'll let your people go. You don't have to stay here any longer.'"

"Did it stop then?" Senefru asked.

"Not exactly," the Hebrew explained. "Moses said that as soon as he left the city he would pray. So he walked out to the edge of the city, lifted his hands, and asked God to make it stop. And, of course, it did."

"Is it pretty bad out there?"

"Horrible. The barley was ripe and the flax was blooming, so they were both flattened. But the wheat crop and the spelt don't come up till later, so I think they'll be all right. But you know what's happened?"

Senefru shook his head, but he had a feeling in the pit of his stomach that Pharaoh had changed his mind again.

"Yeah, the king changed his mind as soon as the hail stopped, and now Moses has told him that there's going to be a plague of locusts and that they're going to eat everything not ruined by the storm."

"How can he keep doing this?" the boy demanded. "Pretty soon even his most loyal servants will revolt against him just to survive."

"Well, I think that's what's happening," the slave said. "The people are already complaining in fear and begging Pharaoh to let us go. Look around. Egypt was the greatest power in the world when we came here. And it's destroyed. The people are sick. And tomorrow they'll have locusts in addition. I can't blame them for rebelling."

Senefru sighed. "There's not much left of Egypt, is there? It's really sad. This was a wonderful place to live."

"Wonderful for you, maybe," Miriam snapped. "It's never been wonderful for us."

The boy glanced at his aunt and fell silent.

And the whole land lay quietly waiting for the swarms coming the following day.

* * *

Senefru stood on the edge of the slave part of town, hardly able to believe his eyes. He could see perfectly in the part of town where the slaves lived, and yet a black wall stood between him and the rest of Egypt. There was no light anywhere. The plague of locusts had come and eaten every shred of green in the entire country. Egypt was now agriculturally crippled with all her animals dead and every growing plant gone. The king had finally relented and the Lord blew the locusts into the Red Sea—just as Pharaoh changed his mind once more. Now God had sent darkness over all the land except where the Hebrews lived.

"I don't understand how He does it," the boy whispered, "but it's wonderful."

Suddenly somebody stumbled through the darkness and fell into the light at Gershom's feet. Senefru dropped to his knees.

"Father!"

Keenan looked terrible. His boils had not healed yet, and he was terribly thin. Bruises and wounds covered him everywhere.

"Did someone beat you up?" his son asked.

Only the man's eyes moved as he shifted his gaze to his son. His neck hurt too much to turn his head. "In a manner of speaking—it was the God of Moses."

Senefru cradled his father's head in his lap. "You'll be fine now," he said. "We'll take care of you. I'll take you to Aunt Miriam's place."

"We've lost everything," his father moaned. "Even our Hebrew cow died. We have no food. And we have no home—it collapsed in the hailstorm. The metalworking shop is gone. And I think I'm dying."

"Don't die, Father," Senefru pleaded, his voice cracking. "Let me get you to Aunt Miriam's house." He picked his father up and carried him as lightly as if he was a lamb back to the tiny one room home that had become a haven for so many lately.

"Keenan!" Mother shrieked when she saw him, then burst into tears. Everyone quickly clustered around him.

"I guess I should have come before," Father said faintly.

"What about the Egyptians?" Mother asked.

"I have no business. Now that Egypt is crushed, I'm finished too."

"Come with us," Moses, who had entered the house, now suggested. "We'll be leaving Egypt soon."

"I don't even have the money to travel now, and I'm too sick," Keenan protested.

The Hebrew leader studied him, then glanced at the others. "If you chose to be on the Lord's side, He'll give you what you need to get out of here."

Keenan's eyes met the older man's. They stared at each other for a long moment. Then Keenan nodded. "I was His once."

Moses knelt by his side. "I know. And you can be His again."

"You really think so?" Keenan asked weakly.

"I do. Now sleep. We have exciting times coming. The darkness will be lifting soon, and we have a few more things to suffer. But not many. We're going to be leaving."

Keenan closed his eyes and soon fell asleep.

* * *

Three days had gone by. Keenan had slept for two of them. Now he was up and walking weakly as Senefru supported him. They met Moses coming from the meeting place in the center of Goshen.

133

"Where are you going, Moses?" Senefru asked.

"To the palace. It's been three days. The pharaoh is tired of the darkness."

"Be careful," the boy said.

Moses smiled. "I have the God of our people, the Nameless One, going before me. I'm not afraid. Neither do you need to be afraid. It's going to be all right." Then he turned toward the palace.

In less than an hour the thick darkness was gone and the sun shone on Egypt again. Or what was left of it.

"You must let us take our animals and all our belongings and go," Moses repeated yet again after he entered the throne room.

"Get out of my sight!" Pharaoh screamed. "Don't come see me again. If you do, you will die."

"I'll do exactly as you have commanded me. I will never step into your sight again."

"Good! Get out! Get out! Go wherever you want to, but you may not have your people and animals. They're my slaves, I tell you. Mine! Besides their animals are the only ones left in Egypt. If you take them, we'll have nothing. Get out! Go back to tending sheep, as you were doing before you began to trouble us."

Moses calmly left, as if oblivious to Pharaoh's raving.

* * *

"Quick, come," one of the leaders of the Hebrews declared. "A representative from every family needs to meet in the square. Moses has an announcement for all of us."

"I will represent my family," Keenan said.

Senefru accompanied him though his father's step was stronger.

When they had all assembled, Moses spoke. "This will be the worst plague that has ever hit Egypt."

An undercurrent of voices swept through the crowd. What could possibly be worse than what they'd already experienced? The one God had already brought Egypt to its knees. What was left?

"The Lord has told me that at midnight He will go through every part of Egypt," Moses explained. "Every oldest son in Egypt will die. The oldest son of Pharaoh who sits on the throne will die. The oldest son of the female slaves who work at their hand mills will die. All the male animals who were born to their mothers among the cattle will die. There will be great wailing all over Egypt. It will be worse than it has ever been and nothing like it will ever be heard again."

"What about us?" one person cried. "What about us?"

"The Lord treats Egypt differently than you," Moses continued. "The one God has told us to kill a lamb and paint its blood on the posts of the door. It will be a sign to Him that all of the firstborns in that home are protected by the blood of the lamb. He will pass over you." Moses then went on to give instructions for the meal that the people were to eat that night.

Back at the tiny house, Aaron and Keenan and Moses together slaughtered the lamb, since more than one family lived in the single room. Carefully they smeared the top of the doorframe and the sides. The women scurried about roasting the lamb and preparing the supper.

"We're going to eat with our shoes on," Moses explained. "We need to be ready to go anytime. When the cry goes out, we must leave."

They had thrown their few belongings into a cart and now sat anxiously waiting. None of them felt hungry enough to eat more than a few bites.

At midnight, just as God had promised, screams shattered the stillness. First someone shrieked in one house, then another, until all of Egypt seemed shredded by cries of anguish and sorrow. It was deafening. Every house in Egypt had experienced a death—except for those with blood on the doorpost. The Hebrews huddled together and shivered in terror as they listened to the shrieks and wails of everyone around them.

But the Almighty kept His promise, and He nestled them all safely in the palms of His hands. They just hadn't followed Him long enough to feel safe and comfortable there.

Soon the word spread that even the firstborn son of Pharaoh was dead. The God of the Hebrews was more powerful than even Pharaoh, who claimed to be Horus incarnate.

"It's time to leave," Moses announced. "Egypt is broken. There's nothing left. Even the pharaoh will not oppose us now. Ask the Egyptians whom you have served to compensate you for your service."

As the newly liberated slaves spilled out into the streets of Egypt, the native Egyptians were happy to give them anything they had left. Gold, jewelry, silver—anything just for them to leave. Pharaoh, too, was relieved to have them gone.

The Hebrews poured toward the east. It didn't seem possible that the Lord had completely defeated Egypt.

Senefru found himself singing praises to the one God along with the others. *I may not be a child of Isaac,* he thought to himself. *But I am a child of Abraham and a child of the most powerful God in the universe.* He grinned to himself, for, after all, he was an oldest son, and hadn't the blood of the lamb saved him just as it had the sons of Isaac?

I smiled, too, wishing he could understand what the blood of the lamb really meant and how it was for more sons than just those of Isaac, or even Abraham. *Someday he'll know,* I thought to myself. And then I couldn't help celebrating with the rest of them for the Almighty is awesome.

TIRZAH

or some reason I had thought that after the miracles the Almighty performed to deliver His people from Egypt, crushing an entire nation and forming a new body of people from that ramshackle bunch of slaves, they would have great respect for Him and would worship and follow Him. It did not to happen. And even though He drowned the Egyptian army in the Red Sea, they still continued to mumble and doubt and have a crisis of faith every time they encountered some small setback.

Now Moses was dead as was his successor Joshua. The children of Israel had made it to the Promised Land. As long as they were faithful to the Most High they were free, but as soon as life got too easy they experienced bouts of backsliding and idolatry. After a while the Lord would withdraw His protection since the people no longer asked for it, and they would suffer at the hands of their neighbors. It happened again and again. Soon I could see it coming even before it occurred.

Now a new king ruled in Hazor. Jabin was the grandson of the king by the same name who was defeated by Joshua. He had a brilliant military commander named Sisera. Jabin had amassed many iron-studded chariots with blades on the wheels that cut people to shreds as they drove through an opposing army. Such a force kept the people of Israel in constant fear.

When the land was settled most of the Kenites, who had traveled to the land of Canaan with the children of Israel, had settled in the southern portion. Although still friendly with the Israelites, they had made alliances with their Canaanite neighbors, adopted some of their religion (though still worshiping the God of Abraham), and usually did not meddle much in local affairs.

Heber was different. Having grown up with the story of Moses and Jethro and the exciting stories of the Exodus and the deliverance, he worshiped the one God more devoutly than most of his people. As some of the family became closer to the Canaanites, the situation became uncomfortable enough for Heber to take his young wife, Jael, and his younger sister, Tirzah, and migrate north.

"I'm going to have to leave for a few days," he told them one morning. "I need to pick up some more copper ingots, then I'll be back." A look of concern crossed his face. "There have been some military raids in the area lately. You must be careful."

Tirzah shuddered as she thought about the warfare between the Canaanites and some of the tribes of Israel.

"Don't worry about that," Jael said, sensing her worry. "We're not Israelites—we're Kenites. And we get along well with the Canaanites. We're in no danger. The quarrel is between the Israelites and the Canaanites, not with us."

The girl nodded. "You've left us alone before and nothing happened."

"Yes, but I never like it. The people in the village will protect you, though."

Tirzah went back into the camp while Heber and Jael chatted about the supplies he needed to purchase. She was proud of her brother. He had set up his own little metal working place. It was much easier to worship the one God further away from the rest of the family. Now she was looking forward to when Heber would be gone. Even though she would miss him, it meant no pumping of the bellows and no hot metal work. She and Jael could catch up on other chores.

* * *

"So what are we going to do today?" Tirzah asked her sister-in-law. "We have two days, and need to plan them out."

Jael laughed. "Let's go to the market. There are some extra things we need."

Laughing and joking, the two headed for the nearest village. They bought some fruit and vegetables from the local farmers and then spent the rest of their time looking at soft fabrics, sniffing exotic spices imported from the East, and examining jewelry brought in by the last caravan. As they passed one stall, they overheard two women talking.

"It's going to be a really big battle this time," the older woman said. "No more hit and run raids. The prophet has called Barak and summoned him to her place of judgment under the palm tree."

"Clear down in Ephraim territory?" the other asked.

"Yes. And she says God told her that he was to attack Sisera's army."

"Barak and a few Ephraimites with no spears and swords against an army of chariots? They will be destroyed!"

"Well," the older woman continued, "you've heard the stories. Apparently the one God has done this kind of thing before. He drowned the entire Egyptian military."

"But that was more than 100 years ago. He doesn't do those kinds of things these days."

The older woman looked at her and raised an eyebrow. "Well, He hasn't recently, but I think something big is about to happen."

A young man interrupted. "Barak's not down in Ephraim anymore. They have pulled together a ragtag army of sorts and have headed toward Kedesh. Apparently they're all meeting there."

"Well, I know the people from Hazor aren't going to join them," the older woman told him. "They're trying to remain neutral in all this. After all, they say it's not their problem."

Tirzah looked at Jael. Their eyes met, then they both looked down. It wasn't their problem either.

"If the one God called for this battle," someone protested, "then it's everyone's problem who worships Him. I think that we should all support anything He tells us to do. Otherwise, when it's our turn no one will be there to protect us either."

An argument broke out.

"Let's go home," Jael whispered. "This isn't fun anymore."

The walk back to their dwelling seemed much longer than the journey into town had been. Their footsteps dragged and conversation lagged as they thought more and more about the things they had heard in the marketplace.

"Do you really think war will break out?" Tirzah asked finally.

"It sure sounded that way. It's one thing for Sisera to continue his raids now and then. But if the prophet has amassed an army, it could lead to a major war."

"But won't they just all be slaughtered?" the girl said. "They don't have a chance."

Jael raised an eyebrow. "Don't ask me. You belong to those who worship the God of the Israelites."

Tirzah nodded. "I know, I know. Heber and I have told you all these wonderful stories about the God of Abraham and Isaac and Jacob and all the things He did. And my grandfather did come out of Egypt with the Israelites. He was there for the 10 plagues and crossed the Red Sea just like the rest of them. It's just that . . . well, he's dead now. It's been a long time, and the idea of all this scares me."

"Scares me, too," Jael replied. "I'm glad Heber will be home in a day or two. In the meantime, it's not our problem."

"But what about the prophet? If God really told her to summon Barak, wouldn't He want all of us to rally behind him?"

"I don't know," Jael sighed. "I really don't know."

* * *

"Jael," Tirzah called. "Someone's coming."

Her sister-in-law slipped out of the tent and stood in the doorway. The man approaching them seemed out of breath. "May I have a drink?" he asked.

"Certainly," Jael replied in the ancient tradition of ancient near eastern hospitality.

She brought him some water and then offered him a bowl of curds, a favorite food of the people of Canaan. The man seemed famished.

"What news do you have?" she said. "Are we at war?"

"We are. The army of Israel has been marching from Mount Tabor. It has 10,000 men, but they're very poorly armed. Sisera is coming down from the north with all of his men and his iron chariots."

"They have not fought yet?"

"No, not yet. I'm delivering a message and have to go. May the one God bless you for your hospitality."

"We have no enemies. We are Kenites."

The man nodded. "May the one God bless you anyway." And he set off down the trail.

"What are we going to do?" Tirzah said, watching the man leave.

"I want you to stay inside the inner tent—and don't come out no matter what happens."

"But why? I'm as strong as you are. If something terrible happens, it will affect both of us."

"And it might," Jael said. "But until I call for you, you must stay inside. You'll be safe in there since no one goes into the inner tent without an invitation. I want you to hide just in case." She poured some water into the cooking pot and started cutting some of the vegetables they had purchased in the market for a stew. "We just have to wait and see what happens."

"I can work at my loom, I suppose."

Tirzah's mother had tried hard to teach her to weave before she had died from the winter illness that had gone through their whole village. The girl had set up the loom in the tent when she had moved with Heber and Jael, but she very rarely touched it. Slowly she sat down in front of it and started to weave the colored yarn through the strands, but her mind was far away.

The afternoon dragged slowly by. Soon the light was too dim for her to continue weaving. She crept over and peeped through the crack in the tent wall. Jael stood absently stirring the pot, staring into the distance. The sky was full of angry dark clouds. Suddenly the earth shook with thunder. Lightning slashed across the sky. Tirzah stared at it in surprise. Since it was past the rainy season, it was unusual for a storm to come this time of year. Was it an omen?

"I need your help," Jael called.

Tirzah scampered out of the tent. Slipping sticks through the handles on each side of the stewpot, they carried it inside the tent. "We can add a lot of things to stew," Jael commented, "but rain isn't my favorite."

Tirzah giggled. "Let's get our cloaks out," she said. "It's cold."

They opened the reed clothing basket and pulled out their winter wool cloaks.

"I wonder how the battle is going," Tirzah said. "Over near Megiddo where they are it doesn't take much rain to turn that whole area into a horrible quagmire."

Jael started to laugh. "Sisera's chariots are probably bogged down by now."

"Maybe this is the Lord's way of taking care of his army," Tirzah suggested.

Her sister-in-law turned quickly and looked at her sharply. "Could it be?"

"I don't know. It's been a long time since the Lord has done anything important publicly, but this could be it."

They sat and watched the lightning for a long time. Then they noticed a figure running in the distance.

"Quick, Tirzah, inside the inner tent," Jael hissed, "and don't you come out."

Tirzah hid inside and crouched behind the basket that stored their clothing.

The man approached closer and closer. He was obviously a high-ranking soldier. Tirzah watched through a tiny slit in the tent as Jael walked toward him.

"Turn aside, my lord," she said. "Don't be afraid. You can come in here."

Tirzah's jaw dropped to her chest. What could Jael be thinking? Tirzah started to pray. "God of Abraham, I'm a child of Abraham, too, even if I'm not a child of Isaac and Jacob. Please be with Jael. Don't let her be so stupid. This is obviously not one of your soldiers. O God of Abraham, please protect us and help us."

The man studied Jael through narrowed eyes. "You are a Kenite," he declared.

"I am."

"The Kenites have long been friends of the Canaanites."

Again she nodded.

"Give me some water to drink," he commanded. "I'm very thirsty. I know that if I drink in your home, your hospitality will protect me, for no one ever betrays someone they have served inside their tent."

"Here," she said, "here's some water—and have some curds to eat."

"May the gods bless you for your hospitality," he said. "Can you hide me? Cover me with something."

Jael took off her winter cloak.

As the soldier lay down near the back of the tent she spread it over him. It hid him completely.

"Stand in the door and guard," he ordered. "If anyone asks you if there's a man here, you tell him no."

Silently Jael went toward the opening and stood quietly looking into the distance.

Where was the rest of the army? She wondered. He was obviously a high-ranking soldier belonging to Jabin's army. Could it be Sisera, the general? She listened carefully, but did not turn back to look at the man. A general would not desert except under most unusual conditions. The only reason he might be fleeing alone was if his whole army had been wiped out. She continued to remain motionless.

Tirzah lay still behind the basket in the inner part of the tent. *I'm stuck here,* she thought. *I can't get out of here because I would have to climb over the sleeping soldier to do that, or pull up the side of the tent and make a noise.* She watched as her sister-in-law stood in the doorway for what seemed like hours. Still no help came. "Please, God of Abraham," Tirzah whispered, "give Jael the wisdom to know what to do. I'm terrified. I don't have any ideas. Please send us a man to protect us. But if you were able to defeat his whole army, then surely you can take care of this one man who's left." As she opened her eyes and peeked through the crack she saw Jael glance over her shoulder at the sleeping soldier. He was snoring softly. Then Jael walked over to another tent and picked up a wooden hammer and a large tent peg. With her mouth set in a determined line she returned to the tent.

Tirzah started to tremble and broke out in a cold sweat. *God of Abraham,* she screamed inside her mind, *help. Please take control of this situation. I'm afraid.*

Jael held the crudely sharpened peg in one hand, stared at it, then crouched over the sleeping man. Raising the hammer with the other, she brought it down. Averting her eyes, Tirzah covered her ears with her hands. The girl heard the man convulse—then silence.

Tirzah crawled out from behind the chest. "Jael!"

Her sister-in-law grabbed her, and they hugged each other fiercely, shaking violently. "I had to," Jael said. "He's an enemy of the one God. It doesn't matter to me that he's an enemy of the Israelites, but I had to do this. Let's cover him up."

They pulled the cloak back over him and dragged the basket chest over in front of him so that no one could see him from outside the tent.

As the two girls crouched in the tent, it seemed like hours before anyone came. Tirzah had fallen asleep with her head on Jael's shoulder. Suddenly she awoke to a sound of voices and Jael wiggling free.

"Stay here," she said before stepping out into the evening dimness.

A soldier approached with several men behind him. "I am back," he said. The two women recognized the voice of the messenger that had passed by earlier. "I am leading the army of Israel with Deborah, the prophet. She's in the chariot." He motioned behind him. Jael peered through the growing darkness.

"Don't be afraid," Deborah told her. "The Lord has been with us, and we've been victorious over Sisera's army. He fled this way and we're looking for him. Have you seen him?"

Jael smiled grimly. "I have," she said. "I can show you whom you are looking for." She motioned. Barak followed her into the tent. Stepping around the large basket chest, she pulled back the winter cape. Barak pulled his sword.

"You don't have to kill him," Jael said. "He's already dead."

Barak slumped in disappointment. Deborah spoke softly behind him. "Barak, it's as the Lord said. I came with you as you requested. But the Lord delivered Sisera into the hand of a woman. There's no great honor coming to you for killing the enemy general. However, there is honor in obeying the Lord's call. And we are victorious."

Taking a deep breath, Barak stepped back. "It is the Lord," he said.

Tirzah stood next to Jael.

The prophet raised her hand. "The one God bless you for what you have done for Him and His people today," she said.

The girl drew a deep breath. She had prayed for a man to rescue them, but God didn't need a man—just someone loyal to Him.

PURAH

urah knew something was wrong as soon as he rounded the oak tree and headed toward his family's home. Smoke filled the air, and a horrible feeling gathered in the pit of his stomach. He broke into a run. His father sprawled motionless face down by the cooking fire in front of the house. Hearing wailing from inside the house, he rushed in. His mother was squatting on the floor, rocking back and forth with her hands over her face.

"Mother, Mother, what happened?"

She pulled her hands away and his stomach lurched up into his throat. Blood covered her face. "They've killed your father," she said.

Putting his arms around his mother, he said, "Come outside. We'll get you some water." Gently he led her out, sat her on a rock under the tree, and wiped her face.

One glance over his shoulder told him that their small vegetable garden she had tended so carefully had been reduced to ashes and a few charred twigs. The few pieces of furniture they had in their house were all smashed. Fragments of their clay pots littered the ground and everything else was gone.

With his sleeve he wiped his mother face, then held her against his chest and rocked her back and forth as she had him when he was a little boy. She had a faraway look as she continued to rock and make strange little crying sounds.

"I hate those Midianites," Purah mumbled under his breath. "I hate them! I hate them! Someday they're going to pay for this. God of Abraham, Isaac, and Jacob, I swear to You that someday I'll make them pay for this." He paused for a moment and glanced around, but there was no one there. And then he said, "God of Abraham, Isaac, and Jacob, help me avenge this. I can't do it on my own. There's so many of them. But I swear I will."

It was early June and time for the wheat harvest. Purah guessed there wouldn't be much of one this year. He couldn't even bring himself to go back to where his father lay in front of the house. What could he do now? He was the only son. Wrapping his cloak around his mother, he said, "Stay here, Mother. I'll be right back."

Having nowhere else to turn, he headed for Gideon's house. He had been working for two years now as a servant to Gideon. Gideon was one of the less important sons of Joash from the Abiezer clan. Their family was one of the most wealthy in the town of Ophrah. With his father gone, Gideon was the only one Purah could think of to turn to. Immediately dropping everything, Gideon brought his other servants back to Purah's house and helped him bury his father and clean up some of the debris.

The following days were so busy they all seemed to run together. Gideon helped Purah move his mother into Joash's family compound. It consisted of a cluster of attached dwellings around a courtyard. They settled her into one of them and the women servants of the family helped care for her.

Purah stayed busy as a personal servant to Gideon while frequently checking on his mother. It made it much easier to do, having her right there. And now that Father was gone and the

Midianites had destroyed everything in their house, it was really the only option.

The boy spent the morning helping Gideon carry baskets of wheat out to their winepress. A small grove of trees hid the winepress located in a large depression. Gideon planned to winnow the wheat, but it wasn't safe to do it out in the open. The Midianites were still raiding everyone's crops, and the little wheat Gideon's family had managed to harvest they must now protect at all cost.

After Purah lowered the baskets down into the pit, Gideon jumped in after them. "I'm going to check on Mother now and work around the compound," the boy said. "Then I'll help you carry everything back to the house."

As Purah sat down next to his mother, another servant passed by. "I couldn't get her to eat anything," the woman said. "Maybe she'll eat for you."

He rubbed his mother's shoulder, then dipped some bread into the stew pot. "Eat, Mother," he said, holding the bread up to her lips.

"See, I knew she'd eat for you," said the servant, returning. "She always does better when you're around."

The boy nodded. It was true. He was hoping she would improve enough that he wouldn't need to feed her. *God of Abraham, Isaac, and Jacob, I know that nobody else prays to You these days,* he thought as he continued to feed his mother, *but my father told me about You. I know that You weren't able to do anything about the Midianites— there's a locust plague of them—but could You please help my mother?*

The God of Abraham didn't seem to be answering so Purah continued to dip stew for her. He figured it would be at least an hour, maybe two, before Gideon would need his help.

"Take your time," he whispered to his mother.

Suddenly he heard footsteps and saw Gideon dash past him. "I'll be right back," Purah said, following his master.

"What's the matter?" he asked Gideon. "Did you need me?"

The man turned and stared at him as if he wasn't even there. "I must—I must fix a meal and a sacrifice. Come with me."

"Sure," Purah replied, looking confused. "Didn't your father already make a daily sacrifice to Baal this morning?"

Gideon paled a little. "Yes, but this one's not for Baal. An angel visited me at the winepress."

Purah looked at him curiously. His mother's mind had never been right since the Midianite raid. They had injured her. But nothing had harmed Gideon. Perhaps he had just been out in the sun too long. "What kind of angel?" he asked.

"An angel of the Lord. He showed up as I was threshing the wheat and told me God was with us." Gideon blushed. "Thinking he was just a man, I sarcastically pointed out that God may have been with us when we left Egypt, but he certainly wasn't with us now or we wouldn't be having all this trouble with the Midianites."

The boy nodded. It was how he felt, too.

"And then he said he was the angel of the Lord. And I—I've got to make a sacrifice right away."

"I'll help you. What do you want to do?"

"We need the newest baby goat from the flock. I'm going to sacrifice him, and I've got to make some bread."

"I'll go get the goat," Purah said.

"Good. I'll make the bread. All the women are out in the fields right now and there's no one here to do it."

The boy grinned to himself. He wondered how good Gideon was at making bread. It couldn't be too hard. People did it all the time.

When he returned from the flock with the baby goat in his arms he could hardly stifle his giggles. Gideon had mixed up some bread dough with an entire ephah (half a bushel basket) of flour. If grain hadn't been so scarce, it would have been funny.

"Here let me help you with that," the boy offered. "Don't put any yeast in it. It's going to take a while just to do all of these. If we pat them out into thin, flat pieces of bread, we can bake them really fast here on the outside of the oven. Look—like this." He showed Gideon how to do it.

"Thanks," his master muttered. "I haven't made much bread before."

"Well, neither have I until recently, but we learn quickly."

Gideon nodded. "I'll go fix the meat, while you finish this up. You're doing a good job."

Purah helped Gideon load the steaming meat and the numerous flat loaves of bread into a large basket. "Do you want help carrying this back?"

Gideon shook his head. "I must go alone." He set out toward the little clump of trees carrying the huge basket. Purah stood watching him for several minutes. Could there really be an angel the winepress? He shook his head. It didn't seem very likely, but he certainly hoped it was true.

A few minutes later Gideon raced back toward the house. "He's gone," he said. "The angel just touched his rod to the tray and fire came down from heaven and burned it all up."

The boy stared at him.

"No, really," Gideon insisted.

"I believe you. I saw the fire."

"From back here?"

Purah nodded.

Gideon seemed to let out his breath all at once. "Then it really was real!"

"Yes, I believe it was real. What did he tell you?"

The man glanced both ways and then whispered, "He told me I was to lead the fight against the Midianites."

Purah dropped the cup he was holding. It clattered on the ground unheeded as he thought, *Ever since the day my father was killed, I swore to the God of Abraham that I would do something about them someday. He has answered my prayer.* Aloud, he said to Gideon, "I'll do whatever you want me to."

His master smiled grimly. "I'm not really sure what we're going to do. At the moment we're only an army of two against the hosts of Midian. It's difficult when the Lord tells you what He wants you to do, but doesn't explain how you're going to do it. Yet I'm certain it was real."

Purah was as confused as Gideon about how they were going to approach the task. They agreed not to say anything to anyone else until God gave them more instructions. Then they returned to the winepress to retrieve their wheat.

I quivered with excitement. As the recording angel I find it terribly frustrating to be able to only watch but not do anything about injustices. For that matter, it's just as difficult to watch these humans, who claim to be God's people, ignoring Him and worshiping Baal, and then blaming Him when they have problems. Yet here was my human whom I had been recording praying to the Mighty One, and now we were going to have action. I could hardly wait to see what would happen next.

A few days later Purah was gathering firewood when Gideon strode by.

"Walk with me," he said. "I think I know what we need to do," the man announced as the boy fell into step with him.

Purah looked at him expectantly.

"My father is a Baal worshiper."

"My father was too," Purah replied. "Even though he told me all the stories of the God of Abraham, we had a Baal in the house, too. My mother always said that we didn't want to make any of the gods unhappy—just in case."

Gideon smiled. "I think we have to get rid of the Baals before the God of Abraham will help us."

"That will make your father really angry."

"I imagine the whole family will be," Gideon replied. "As far as I know I'm the only one interested in the God of Abraham. Our whole clan used to be, but that was a long time ago."

"So what are we going to do?"

"We need to take a couple of bulls up to the high place to help us pull down the altar to Baal. Also, we need to chop down the grove around it and the Asherah pole that goes with it, and burn them."

"It'll be hard to do that very secretly," Purah said cautiously.

"I know," Gideon replied grimly. "So I guess it would be safer to do it at night."

"I will if you will."

His master smiled. "I appreciate your loyalty. You know you could get into trouble for this when the rest of my family finds out."

Purah gulped. In fact, it was more likely that his punishment would be more severe since he was a servant. The boy couldn't imagine any of Gideon's family putting up with that, but he didn't care. He had asked the God of Abraham for help and perhaps He would come to their aid now. "I'm with you," he said. "I guess it's all or nothing for us."

"I hope He's paying attention," Gideon commented.

I almost laughed out loud. They had no idea how close the God of Abraham was watching them. Silly humans.

* * *

Purah felt dizzy and sick at his stomach. The shouting mob had dragged Gideon from his house.

"That's him. I saw him last night," someone shouted.

Glancing in the direction of the voice, Purah saw that it was Ehud, one of Gideon's 10 servants. The boy stared at him hard. How could someone named after a godly judge of Israel be so disloyal to his master.

They dragged Gideon up to the high place, the rest of his family rushing along with the mob. Purah followed. So far no one had mentioned him. Finally Joash, Gideon's father put his hand up for silence and turned to his son. "Did you do this terrible thing?" he demanded.

Gideon looked around him. A huge stone altar lay shattered on the ground with ashes and the charred remains of the grove around it. He jutted his chin a little higher. "I did," he said. "The God of Abraham has always been the God of our people. We have no business worshiping Baal or Asherah." Shouting drowned out the rest of his statement.

Purah felt terrible. Should he step forward and say he was involved? Or should he remain silent and thus give his approval to what was happening?

"Burn him like he did the sacred grove. If he burns sacred things, he should burn, too."

The crowd quickly picked up the chant. "Burn him! Burn him! Burn him!" Purah shuddered. It was the worst way he could imagine to die.

Gideon's father put his hand up for silence again. "Why do you people want to waste your time burning this man?"

"Because he profaned our sacred places," someone shouted.

"Wait! Wait!" Joash protested. "Don't we believe that Baal is all powerful."

"Yes, yes," the crowd roared its assent.

"Well, let Baal take out his revenge on him. I'm sure he can punish him much more effectively than any of you. Why don't we stand back and see what Baal does?"

"Yes, let Baal do it. Gideon is in trouble now!" the crowd shouted. But nothing happened.

"Maybe," Joash suggested, "Baal needs some time. But if he's the most powerful god in Israel, he'll be able to punish my son better than I ever could."

The crowd reluctantly agreed with him. "From now on let's call him Jerub-baal ["Let Baal deal with him"]," someone exclaimed.

Purah grinned. He was pretty sure Baal wouldn't do anything, but if there was a god named Baal, Purah certainly hoped that the God of Abraham was stronger and could protect Gideon.

Still nothing happened in the days that followed. More and more people became convinced that perhaps Baal couldn't do anything about Gideon. First, members of the clan of Abiezer and then from the tribe of Manasseh came to join Gideon. People from the other northern tribes soon followed. Gideon hardly knew what to do. Even though he and Purah had a good 15-year age difference they had become close friends, and Purah seemed to be the only one Gideon could really confide in.

"I don't know what to do next," he told the boy. "The God of Abraham has taken care of me and I wasn't killed for tearing down Baal's altars, but I don't know what to do now. Although I have a whole army who's volunteered, I don't know how to lead them. As the youngest son, I've never been in charge of anything except household servants. The most important thing I've ever done was just moving you and your mother in here and taking care of you."

Purah understood—he'd never done anything important either.

"I think the Lord wants me to take this army and attack the Midianites. That's what the angel mentioned that day."

"You have a whole army now. Surely that's the doing of the God of Abraham. How else could you raise an army in the middle of all this?"

"But how do you plan an attack? I've never done anything like this, except when we were playing war games as children."

"Why don't you do it that way?" Purah suggested. "You used to always win."

Gideon chuckled. "Nobody ever died, though. It wasn't the life of my family we were talking about then. We need some kind of a sign."

"A sign? After that huge flash of fire and God sending you an army, you need a sign?"

"Well, just to be sure," Gideon protested.

Purah could understand. It was a frightening decision to make. A sheep bleated somewhere in the distance.

"This is what I'll do," Gideon finally decided. "I'm going to lay a fleece out overnight. In the morning if it's wet and the ground around it is dry, I'll know that God wants me to go ahead with this."

"That's a good idea. By tomorrow you'll know for sure."

Purah could hardly sleep that night. "God of Abraham," he whispered, "I hope You're watching. Please give Gideon the sign he needs because none of us really want to attack the Midianites. We're outnumbered. But I know if You're on our side, we will triumph." Finally he fell into a dreamless sleep.

When morning came he rushed out the door to find Gideon. "Did you find out what you needed to know?" he asked.

Gideon didn't look near as excited. As soon as they were out of earshot, Purah asked, "What's the matter? Wasn't the fleece wet?"

"It was soaking wet."

"Then I don't understand. You have your sign. It's time to fight."

"Well, what if it's just because that's the way fleece is—you know, the ground was dry, but it absorbed all the moisture in the air. I mean, fleece can do that."

Purah's shoulders sagged. "So we still aren't sure."

"Either that or we're just scared."

"Do you think that the God of Abraham would get angry if you asked one more time?" the boy suggested. "I mean, we don't want to make Him mad, but do you think He would do it the opposite way? Leave the fleece bone-dry and the ground around it all soaked with dew?"

Gideon looked happier. "I'll ask Him. I hope it doesn't make Him angry, but Moses did write that He was long-suffering and slow to anger. We'll wait till tomorrow. If we have our sign then, there'll be no more excuses."

"Tomorrow then," Purah agreed and headed back toward his other chores.

* * *

Purah felt overwhelmed. He'd never been in such a huge crowd before. At the foot of Mount Gilboa waited 32,000 men, all ready to fight with Gideon. The boy felt honored that he and Gideon were good friends.

Gideon stood with his eyes closed. What was the matter? Was he praying? He opened his eyes and spoke. "I thank all of you for being here today. And I know you have come here not out of loyalty to me, but to the one God, the great I Am, the God of our fathers, Abraham, Isaac, and Jacob. Before we go further, you need to know something. The Midianites outnumber us by about four to one. The Lord spoke to me and told me to allow anyone who is afraid, to leave now. You may leave without dishonor."

Murmuring rippled through the crowd. Purah could not believe his ears. How could Gideon let anyone go? If they were already outnumbered four to one, what was the God of Abraham thinking?

Then men started leaving. Not one at a time, but in droves. Two thirds of the army evaporated in just a few short minutes. Gideon stood silently watching them leave. Then to those who remained, he announced, "Come. Let's head for the brook. A thirsty army isn't going to be very effective."

He watched as they swarmed across the plain. Some of the men scooped up water as they went, crossing the brook and heading for the other side. Others sat down as if it were a picnic and drank slowly, chatting and taking their time. Purah hurried across the brook.

When everyone was finished, Gideon declared, "Those of you who scooped up water as you crossed come to me. But those of you who knelt and took your time to drink stand over there."

The men separated. More than half of them were clustered on one side. "Now those of you who knelt to drink return to your homes."

Hardly able to believe his ears, Purah tugged at Gideon's sleeve. "But, sir, that leaves only about 300."

Gideon nodded curtly. "That's right."

Purah shrugged. He could get killed just as easily being out-numbered four to one as 400 to one. In the long run, it wouldn't matter. But if they were to win, it would definitely be an act of God, because 300 men could do nothing against the Midianite hordes.

"Now," Gideon said, "gather as close as you can. Here's the plan."

* * *

It was the evening before the attack. Purah had spent all after-noon distributing the supplies—a large clay pitcher and a torch tipped with pitch—to each man. Very few had swords or spears, but they all came with their farm tools. He returned to the tent where Gideon was resting.

"Is that it?" he asked. "Is there anything else?"

"Yes. Come with me. I'm going to scout the Midianite camp. I need to know what they're doing."

Purah was too excited to sleep anyway.

The two men crept through the darkness, slipping past the sen-tries posted around the camp and crawling up next to a tent. They could hear two Midianite soldiers talking inside.

"What is the matter with you? I never heard you yell in your sleep like that before," one of them said to the other.

"I had the most horrible nightmare. I just have such a bad feel-ing about this raid."

"Why? What did you dream?" the first asked.

"I dreamed that a loaf of barley bread from up on the hill rolled down. It went faster and faster, and when it got to our tents, it just crushed them all."

"You're afraid of a loaf of bread?" the other replied sarcastically.

"No," the second man said. "It's a symbol. Those children of Israel grow barley. That's what they eat—barley loaves. I told you I had a bad feeling about this."

Gideon glanced in Purah's direction. They smiled in the darkness and then crept back up the hill. Purah took a deep breath. Surely the God of Abraham was with them. He had helped Gideon plan his tactics and he was even giving nightmares to the Midianites.

It was well after midnight when the two spies returned to the camp.

"Spread the word," Gideon announced. "We attack in two hours."

Silently the men formed their ranks. Just before they left they lit their torches and pulled the large clay pots down over them. The torches smoldered but didn't go out. When they removed the pot the torch would burst into flame with the sudden rush of air.

Purah's heart pounded in his chest and he felt as if he could hardly breath. He was in the second company with Gideon. Company one was to the left and company two was on their right. And the Midianites spread out below them in the valley.

As he stood next to Gideon, Purah almost wanted to laugh out loud at the brilliant plan. Usually only the captain of a company carried a torch and all the men behind him would follow the light. The story his father had told him about capturing Jericho had been fascinating, and he remembered that only seven priests carried trumpets. Yet each man in Gideon's army carried a shofar that they would blow a blast on. The Midianites would think that instead of the 300 men they would have 300 bands of men, an army of at least 30,000. Purah grinned and then became more serious. Still—and the boy instantly sobered—once the Midianites found out their actual numbers, 300 men didn't stand much of a chance.

Gideon had his eyes closed as if in prayer. Then he drew a deep breath and smashed the clay pot on the ground. His torch flared up and he blew a loud blast on his shofar. Immediately, all of the men with him shattered their pitchers on the ground and blew their horns. The sound was deafening and the whole valley seemed alight.

Suddenly pandemonium broke loose in the Midianite camp. The soldiers, still bleary-eyed, staggered out of their tents.

"We're being attacked," they shouted. Drawing their weapons, they lashed out at the nearest person.

Gideon's army stood in awe on the hills surrounding the Midianites as they watched the entire Midianite army slaughter each other. A few of them escaped to the south, and Gideon's bands trooped after them, grabbing up Midianite weapons as they went, in the process becoming a well-armed force.

As Purah ran to keep up with Gideon he shouted into the night air, "Thank You, God of Abraham. It's just like the stories. You really are mighty. And now if You would just help my mother." A flood of peace and joy came over him.

JARED

ared halted hesitantly at the edge of the circle of young people. "Welcome to the school of the prophets," a friendly voice said. "You may stand here with Ethan and do what he does until our classes finish for today."

Nodding, Jared glanced shyly at Ethan. The other boy grinned back. Tall and lanky with unruly curly black hair that would not stay under his head covering, he looked friendly. Jared felt relieved. Going to be a student in one of the schools of the prophets had sounded exciting when his father had first mentioned it at home, but the closer they came to Ramah, the smaller and less brave he felt. As his father left, Jared could hardly keep from running after him and begging to go home to Nob.

"Come with me," Ethan instructed as soon as class finished. "I'll show you where we sleep and where you can put your things."

Jared looked down at his satchel. His possessions consisted of an extra outer robe and a few loaves of bread that his mother had tucked into the bag as he was leaving—and his mantle. He was especially proud of his mantle. The tassels on the corners had the blue thread in them to remind him of the covenant between God and His people.

"Was that the prophet Samuel teaching the class we were just in?" he asked Ethan.

The other boy laughed. "No, Samuel is a really old man. It would wear him out to teach us every day. We study the things he plans for us, but he has some specially trained Levites who do the actual teaching. You will get to meet him, though. He travels between the two schools and speaks with us sometimes."

"What does the prophet give you to study?"

"We must memorize the sacred texts, plus he has some guidelines for managing the kingdom. My grandfather says he really wrote them for King Saul, back when he was a new king, but Saul never used them."

"Why not?" Jared asked.

"Well, for one thing, at least according to Grandfather, Saul felt that since he was the king, he shouldn't have to accept instructions from anybody."

"Even God's prophet?" Jared said incredulously.

"I guess not. Samuel started the schools of the prophets so that we would be educated and then return to our home towns and teach others how God wanted our country to be run and how our people should live."

"What kinds of things do we learn?" Jared continued.

"Besides having to learn to read and write, we study music and law and sacred history. I have heard that the prophet is writing a book of sacred history now, too."

"Do you think we will get to read it?" Jared, still full of questions, inquired.

"I'm sure we will *have* to read it if he finishes it before we leave school," Ethan laughed.

"I can't wait to meet Samuel! I have heard so much about him."

"Don't let him fool you," Ethan whispered. "He looks like a frail little old man, but he isn't. When he is angry and fixes those flashing eyes on you, it's really frightening. Even King Saul wilts under his fiery gaze." After glancing around quickly, Ethan then added under his breath, "And my father says that he once chopped a king's head off!"

Jared's eyes widened. I shook my head. I just hate it when humans tell a little bit of a story and don't include enough information. It always makes God or His prophets look harsh when there's so much more involved.

I remember that day clearly. Saul had led his armies against the Amelikites. God had told him to kill them all and not to bring back prisoners or booty. Instead, Saul returned with King Agag in chains and lots of animals, women, and other spoil from the Amelikites. Samuel went to where Saul had Agag kneeling in chains and confronted Saul's disobedience. The king protested that he had brought back all the sheep from the Amelikite camp for extra sacrifices to God. The Almighty One didn't believe it and neither did Samuel. He strode over to King Agag and cut his head off, shocking everyone present into silence.

To Saul, it had seemed a minor thing, especially since he just wanted to do things his own way. It added to his prestige to show off the enemy king in chains, and it made him popular with his army to let them take booty home. He was more interested in power and popularity that obeying God.

I was glad that Samuel was recording Israel's history so that someday perhaps people would understand how loving the Mighty One really is and how wise and ultimately merciful even his sternest instructions really are. In the meantime, I guess—as always—humans just have to trust Him.

Jared settled in well at the school. The boy enjoyed his friendship with Ethan and found adjusting much easier with someone to help him. He enjoyed all of his classes and was used to hard work. His favorite class was music. Not only did they perform the old songs used for generations by the followers of God, but they were also learning new contemporary music, including some of the songs that the newest court musician had just composed. His name was David.

"Do you know anything about this David?" Jared asked Ethan one day.

His friend laughed. "Well, sure, I know everything."

Jared believed that it was probably true. Ethan seemed to be a wealth of information and his father seemed to have all kinds of connections. As a result, Ethan knew all the latest rumors circulating through the kingdom.

"So what's he like?" Jared insisted.

"Well, he's the youngest son in his family, so he's never been very important. He spent most of his time herding sheep. His older brothers are important, though. They're soldiers in Saul's army."

"Yes, yes, but tell me about David."

"Well, I guess that all the time he spent sitting out there watching the sheep he used to compose music. A harpist, he would sing his psalms and prepare music for them, and apparently has found

King Saul to be a more appreciative audience than the wooly ones he started out with."

Jared laughed. He could just picture in his mind David surrounded by sheep listening to his concert.

"Well, I really like his hymns," Jared continued. "That one we were learning yesterday is so beautiful. 'The heavens are telling the glory of God and the sky that His hands created them.' I just love the words. Last night I looked up at the stars and they do remind us of God's glory. David is right."

"I like the music better."

"No, no," Jared protested. "It's the words. That part about the law of the Lord being perfect and giving us strength and that we can trust them—it's beautiful."

Ethan shrugged. He was more interested in sharing information about David than in singing his songs.

"I think David is one of the wisest people alive," Jared continued.

"Why do you say that?"

"Well, look at the words to the psalm that he wrote to comfort the king. When the king gets in such a dark mood, I just don't see how he could be discouraged after he listened to the words of David's psalm."

"What one was that? I guess I wasn't paying attention."

Jared shook his head. How could Ethan have missed it? "I'll sing it to you." And he sang, "Lord, the king is filled with joy because You are strong. How great is his joy because You help him win his battles. You have given him what his heart longed for. You haven't kept back from him what his lips asked for."

"You really think that makes the king happy? I hear he has a love-hate relationship with the Lord."

"He does?" Jared asked in surprise.

"Well, that's what my father says. Saul likes to be in charge, and every once in a while he acts as if being the king allows him to make his own decisions instead of waiting to see what the Lord tells him to do through Samuel—especially if the prophet keeps him waiting."

Jared shook his head. "Well, I still like the song. Remember the part that says if the king trusts in the Lord, the faithful love of the Most High will keep him secure?"

His friend laughed. "Well, maybe that's why the king isn't secure, because he doesn't trust in the Lord that much."

"Well, I still think it's a wonderful psalm, and if I was the king and feeling depressed, I would find it very comforting."

"You know what I think?" Ethan offered. "I think that if Saul doesn't really trust in the Lord and David keeps singing to him about Him, one of these days the king is going to just throw something at him."

"I can't believe that will ever happen," Jared scoffed.

"Just my guess. You never know. Saul has a pretty hot temper."

"Really?"

"Oh, yes," Ethan insisted. "He throws things when he's mad. My father said so."

Jared shook his head in puzzlement. Having never lived near the court, he had always viewed King Saul with awe bordering on reverence. It was hard to imagine him as a person with a temper and good days and bad days like everyone else. "It worries me that Saul doesn't follow God with his whole heart."

Ethan gave him a sharp look.

"Well, it has always been that when we followed God and our leaders followed God, we did well. When our leaders didn't follow God, terrible things happened."

"Perhaps," Ethan said slowly, "if enough of us in Israel are loyal to God, God will bless Israel even if our king is not what we wish he was."

Jared had a faraway look in his eye. It was something he needed to think about.

The other boys at the school of the prophets referred to Jared and Ethan as "Why" and "Who." Ethan was "Who." Always full of the latest gossip, he knew who was doing what and with whom and seemed to have sources everywhere. They named Jared "Why," because he was always asking questions. And today was no different.

"Why," he asked the priest who was instructing them, "are we learning so much about the sanctuary and Moses' rules for that when we don't have one. What happened to the wilderness sanctuary we've been studying about?"

The priest stroked his beard for a moment as he tried to think of the most diplomatic way to phrase his answer. "It happened only a few years ago," he said finally. "The high priest then was Eli. He raised the prophet Samuel."

"Was Samuel his son?"

The priest shook his head. "No. Samuel was the son of a Levite named Elkanah and a woman named Hannah. Since the woman had been barren for many years and Samuel was an answer from God to her prayers for a child, she dedicated him to the Lord. His mother brought him to the sanctuary as soon as he was weaned and then Eli took charge of him."

"That doesn't explain what happened to the sanctuary, though," Jared observed.

"Oh, yes, the sanctuary," the priest said, getting back to the point. "We were already at war with the Philistines. Eli's two sons, Hophni and Phinehas, thought that if we carried the ark of the covenant into battle as other nations do their symbols of their gods, our God would fight on our side."

"Did they ask God's permission first?" Jared questioned.

"No. They had a history of treating God and His things with disrespect. This was just one incident of many. They took the ark into battle. At first it frightened the Philistines, but, unfortunately, once they recovered from their fear, they slaughtered us—well, not all of us," the priest said, beginning to shift from one foot and to the other, obviously uncomfortable. "Hophni and Phinehas both perished and the Philistines captured the ark. They swarmed back to Shiloh and destroyed the sanctuary. That's why we don't have one now."

"So all the stuff we studied about the Day of Atonement and all those other things can't happen right now," Jared observed, half as a question, half as a statement to himself.

"Yes, yes, but the ark is still with us. In Nob, where you come from, we still offer sacrifices to the Lord. But you're right—we don't really have a full-fledged sanctuary right now."

Jared's forehead wrinkled. "But why—why haven't we done something about it? Saul is our king. Why isn't he doing something about it?"

The priest now started to stutter. "Well—well, you see Saul—Saul may not care about that right now. He—he has other things to think about. Fighting the Philistines, running the country."

"But surely worshiping God properly would be more important than battling the Philistines or anything else."

"It's enough questions for today," interrupted an elderly priest who had just arrived. "We need to get on with other things. Let's move on to a music lesson."

The boy frowned.

The student behind him snickered. "Aren't you going to ask why we're going to do a music lesson? You ask why for everything else."

Blushing, Jared said nothing.

Jared had been at the school of the prophets almost a year when his father showed up one day. "I'm sorry, Jared," he said. "I know that you really enjoy school and I believe that it's where God wants you to be, but I need you to help me."

"What's happening?" he asked. "Is anything wrong with Mother?"

"You're mother is fine," his father said, smiling gently. "The Philistines have been raiding again."

"Yes, we're always at war with the Philistines."

"Well, it's a big battle and we're all going and I need you to come, too."

Jared understood. Several of the other boys were leaving the schools of the prophets to join the battle, too

Although his father had taught him a few military skills, Jared had never been in a real battle. Now he would really see the Philistines. He hoped he would act bravely.

It was hard saying goodbye to his friend Ethan and the others, but it was too exciting to grieve over for long.

When they reached the battle site Jared's father quickly found the rest of his family. They had a quick lunch and then went out to the edge of the valley. The Israelites had lined up on one side, the Philistines on the other. Both armies waited for the other to make the first move. Suddenly Jared noticed a stirring on the Philistine side. The boy and his friends jostled each other, trying to see what was going on. A huge man strode out into the center of the valley.

"You men of Israel," he shouted. "There's no point in all of us getting killed. I am Goliath of Gath. I will represent the Philistines. Send me out your best soldier and we'll fight. Whichever one of us wins, the other side will submit. I know none of you are in the mood for dying today, anyway. You Israelites are all cowards."

Cowards! Jared bristled at the idea.

As Goliath continued talking, his insults and taunts became more and more offensive.

"How can he say those things?" Jared protested. "That's blasphemy. Are we just going to stand here and let him talk like that?"

"I am," his father replied. "How about you?"

"But—but he's blaspheming our God."

"Yes, but what are we going to do about it? Do you want to fight anybody that size? I'll bet his spear weighs as much as you do."

His son stared for a moment. "Yes, it probably does."

"Well?" his father continued.

"Never mind. I'll be quiet now." Jared stared at his feet. He couldn't understand why no one would battle the Philistine. Yet he was afraid to.

Goliath paced up and down the valley, heaping insult upon insult on the armies of Israel and particularly their God.

Suddenly a young man walked from the Israelite side toward the Philistine battle line.

"He's not very big either," Jared pointed out to his father.

"No, and we'll just stand here and watch him get slaughtered."

Although Jared felt sick to his stomach, he couldn't tear his eyes away from the scene.

The smaller man approached the giant, unafraid.

"Come here, little man," Goliath boomed. "I'm going to feed you to the birds."

"No, you're not," the younger man shouted in reply. "You come to me with a sword and a spear, but I come to you in the name of the Lord." He pulled something from his small skin satchel and tucked it into his sling.

"What do you think I am?" the giant bellowed. "A dog? Will you throw rocks at me? Think I'll run home with my tail between my legs because you hurled a rock or two?"

The younger man didn't answer but released the stone through the air. It hit the giant right in the forehead. He dropped to the ground. The Israelite ran forward, grabbed the huge sword from the giant, and with one blow chopped his head off. Seizing it by the hair, he held it high. The armies of Israel roared. The Philistines scattered. Jared ran with the rest of the army after them, picking up the weapons they dropped along the way.

That night around the campfire everyone was too excited to sleep.

"Who was that?" Jared asked someone.

"That was David, son of Jesse. He was a shepherd until last year. Since then he's been at court as Saul's musician."

"The musician? The one who writes those psalms? The one that wrote the hymn about—"

"Yes, yes, that's him," said one of the other men.

"Oh." Jared remembered a rumor that Ethan had passed along. Something about the prophet Samuel anointing a new king. Could this David be the same one? Surely Samuel wouldn't anoint someone else as king while the current one was still on the throne. The boy frowned. Why would Samuel do that? Could it be that the prophet was feeling old and wanted to anoint the next king before he died? No, that couldn't be. Saul had a son who was a great war hero. Everyone knew that Prince Jonathan was going to be the next king. Jared shook his head. Some things were too hard to figure out.

* * *

Jared and his father went home to Nob after the battle. He enjoyed telling others about the huge giant and the young soldier who had killed him without any armor or weapons of his own except for a shepherd's sling.

At first rejoicing spread all through the land and the women sang everywhere about the new hero David. One tune compared David with King Saul. The chorus went "Saul has killed his thousands, but David his ten thousands." Jared wondered how that would go over with King Saul. From the stories Ethan had told him it sounded as if the king did not tolerate the idea of a rival. The boy hoped that David would be safe.

It wasn't long before stories began filtering out from Gibeah that David's life was in danger. In fact, Saul was trying to kill him.

One day Jared was just heading back toward his home with a load of firewood when he saw someone approaching the town. He had to take a second look to be sure—but it was David. He dropped the firewood and ran toward him.

"We're honored you've come to our town," he said.

The visitor smiled nervously. "I thank you, young man," he said. "I'm honored to meet you. My name is David. I've come to see the priest Ahimelech. I need him to ask the Lord what I should do next."

Jared nodded. Ahimelech was high priest even if Israel no longer had Moses' tabernacle. He had set up a tent for the ark, and still fixed the weekly shewbread and offered sacrifices, praying for the sins of his people.

"I'll show you where he lives," Jared offered. "Come with me."

The boy hung around, knowing that he really needed to get back to his firewood, but not wanting to miss any excitement. Because David talked quietly with Ahimelech, Jared couldn't hear a thing, only the rising and falling of their voices. But he could sense that the high priest seemed afraid.

Then David said, "Thank you so much. Also, do you have any bread? My men and I are hungry."

"No," Ahimelech said after a pause. "Only the shewbread. But it's for the Lord," the high priest protested. "Only men who have not touched women can eat that."

"It's really an emergency," David insisted. "My men are starving. And they are pure. When we are facing battles and danger, we commit ourselves to the Lord—and none of us have seen our wives for days."

At last Ahimelech gave David the bread.

"God will bless you for this," his visitor said.

The high priest said nothing.

"One more thing. Do you have a sword?"

"One," Ahimelech answered. "I have the sword from the giant

you killed." He disappeared into a tent, then returned with something wrapped up in a cloth. Removing the cloth, he revealed an enormous sword, then handed it to David. "God bless you and protect you," he said. "And now you must go."

As Jared slowly returned to his abandoned firewood he noticed Doeg, the Edomite. The boy frowned. He didn't know Saul's chief of shepherds very well, but Ethan had told him not to trust him. Jared shook his head. Ethan was always full of gossip. Maybe his friend just didn't like him because he was an Edomite. Still the boy had a funny feeling in the pit of his stomach.

Jared had become friends with Abiathar, another former student at the school of the prophets, though he had been there some time before Jared had attended. The young man was also Ahimelech's son. He and Abiathar were together the afternoon that Saul and his men galloped into town. They all bowed in awe. Why would the king of Israel choose to come to a small town like Nob? Had he come to consult with the high priest? By this time everyone knew that the king paid very little heed to what God or His priest thought. So why was he here now?

But Jared was too busy being scared to ask the question out loud. "We need to hide, Abiathar," he whispered.

"But I want to see what the king is here for," his friend protested.

"Something bad is going to happen, I know it."

Jared glanced around him. His eyes rested on Doeg, the Edomite, now riding just a few paces behind the king. "Follow me," the boy insisted. "I'll tell you what I think is going to happen."

As the king and his men thundered past and headed for Ahimelech's home, Jared and Abiathar fled in the other direction. They ran until they were out of breath. In a gully south of town they hid in a little cave they had once played in.

"It's Doeg," Jared said, "that Edomite. He was here the day David was here. I've heard that the king and David are not getting along. I think Saul is after him and I believe something bad is going to happen here. I just don't trust him."

Abiathar laughed. "Jared, you have the wildest imagination. I'm going back. You brought me out here just because you had a bad feeling?"

"I didn't have a bad feeling—I just know it."

"Come on, we're gonna miss all the excitement. The one day the king comes to town you drag me off to a cave because you have a bad feeling."

Abiathar turned on his heel and headed back toward town. Jared sat down and rested his head on his knees. Maybe he was being stupid. It was all Ethan's fault. He sat trying to figure it out. Why? Why? His questions kept going round and round inside his head. Would the Lord explain things to him?

"Are You there?" he whispered in the darkness of the cave. "God of Abraham, if You're listening to me—and Samuel taught us that You are always listening—please help me to understand. I just can't go back there right now."

The boy received no answer, but soon felt a little more peaceful. Lulled by the silence of the cave, he fell asleep.

* * *

"Jared, Jared, wake up."

He startled awake. Where was he? Oh, yes, the cave. "What's the matter?" he asked.

It was Abiathar—shaking and sobbing.

"What happened? What's wrong?"

It was a few moments before his friend could answer. "Jared, you were right. It's horrible. It's just horrible. They're all dead."

"Who's dead?"

"I didn't get back there in time, so I saw some of this from a little distance. I guess Saul was looking for David. He knew my father, Ahimelech, helped David. As I got closer I could hear him protesting that while he had helped David and given him food and a sword, David was a loyal subject just like anyone else and loyal to Saul. The king wouldn't hear of it and commanded one of his men to kill my father. That's when I hid. I'm ashamed. The rest of the priests came out and stood with Ahimelech—all of them."

"All of them?" Jared echoed. "Even my father?"

Abiathar nodded. "The soldier refused to kill a priest of God. Saul went down the line. None of the soldiers would do it. But Doeg the Edomite—"

"Doeg! I knew it!" Jared exploded. "He killed your father?"

"Worse than that," Abiathar sobbed. "He killed everyone."

"Everyone?" Jared repeated. "Everyone—our fathers—everyone?"

"More than that," Abiathar continued. "They went through the town. They killed the women and the babies and the children— even the flocks. He murdered everyone."

Jared was stunned. "If I hadn't felt that something was wrong, I wouldn't have come to hide in the cave," he said slowly.

Abiathar nodded. "Yes, and if you hadn't dragged me off here, I wouldn't have gotten there late and had another chance to hide."

"What do we do now?" Jared asked. "We have no family. What will we do?"

"Well, I don't know about you, but I don't feel loyal to King Saul anymore. God's prophet might have anointed him king, but Saul's turned his back on God. And I want to turn my back on him."

His feelings all confused, Jared remained silent. He didn't feel as if he could even stand, much less think.

"I know where David is," Abiathar announced.

"You do?"

"Yes. Ahimelech did too. He just didn't tell. I'm going to join him. While I'm not a soldier, he may need a Levite or two around. I have one of the ephods. At least we can sing his songs for him."

Jared thought for a moment, then declared. "I'm with you."

Jared and Abiathar traveled by night, hiding in fear from everyone they encountered. But no one was looking for the two young men.

"You know," Abiathar said one day, "I think my father guessed something like this might happen."

"What makes you think that?"

"It was one of Samuel's first prophecies to Eli. God told him that none of our family were going to live to be old men."

Jared considered it, then nodded. "Hophni and Phinehas died in battle."

"Well, that was probably a good thing for all of Israel. They were terrible."

Jared sighed. "They even had Egyptian names. Hophni means tadpole. And I'm told Phinehas means Nubian, but there wasn't anything Nubian about him."

"Yes. I wonder why Eli gave them foreign names when he was a priest of God—the high priest even?"

"So what were you saying about Eli's family?"

"Well, my father was the last one of Eli's relatives. Now they're all dead except for me."

"But Eli was a Levite. We're all his relatives."

"Right," said Abiathar. "But of his close family I'm the last one."

Jared shook his head. "So God knew and told Samuel way back then that this was going to happen."

"Yes. Somehow it makes me feel a little better. If the God of Israel knew what was going to happen even down to the last relatives of Eli and told Samuel so long ago, I think we can trust the other things he told the prophet. I think if we follow Him with all our heart and do all the things we learned in Samuel's school of the prophets, I think He'll take care of us."

Then Jared frowned again. "But what about you? And Saul?"

"What about us?" Abiathar said bitterly.

"Well, does the prophecy apply to you, too? And Ethan told me that Samuel anointed someone to be a new king when Saul dies."

Abiathar sighed. "I don't know. I will just have to trust God. And who do you think will be the new king?"

"I believe it will be David. Rumor has it that it happened before David went to court to be the musician for Saul and way before his encounter with Goliath."

"You and I are ready to follow him anyway," Abiathar said. "But it makes sense that he might be the one chosen by God."

"But part of it I don't understand," Jared continued. "If Saul dies, Jonathan will be king. I don't see how David could become king without—"

"Overthrowing Saul?" Abiathar suggested.

"Perhaps, but that doesn't seem to be God's way of doing things."

The priest's son shook his head. "No, but sometimes God fights our battles for us. Remember all the stories about how God went ahead of our people as we entered Canaan and sometimes drove people out with hornets and sometimes knocked their walls down without us doing a thing. Maybe God knows something we don't know about how Saul is going to end up."

"I don't know. But for now I'm going to join David, and, like you, I'm going to have to trust God. After all, He seems to understand what's going on—I certainly don't."

"I don't either," Abiathar sighed. "But one thing I know, in this whole crazy conflict, we can always trust Him."

I smiled. Here were two of the wisest humans on their little planet. Trusting the Mighty One was the only thing they could do in such confusing times. Times when all their rules about worship couldn't be followed because their sanctuary had been partially destroyed. No matter how confused the survivors of this dark conflict might become, they could always trust the Mighty One.

EPILOGUE

ared and Abiathar joined David and his band of friends at Keilah. Life wasn't easy, but because they had no family to return to, it was their best option. They remained loyal to God and to David, though Saul and his armies hunted and chased them. It was only two years later that Saul and his son Jonathan died fighting the Philistines. All three of Saul's sons perished that day. And just as the prophet Samuel had anointed him so many years before, David became the king of Israel. Jared became a priest and taught in one of the schools of the prophets that Samuel had started, and Abiathar became high priest of Israel. David was loyal to the Mighty One. He had the ark of the covenant brought from the home where it had sat idle all those years. They put together a sanctuary for it in Jerusalem. And David began the plans for building the greatest building project anyone could ever imagine—a huge temple to the Almighty. His son Solomon would actually construct it. Though the conflict continued, the survivors were always those who stayed loyal and trusted the Mighty One.